COPING WITH CULTURAL
and RACIAL DIVERSITY
in URBAN AMERICA

'COPING WITH CULTURAL and RACIAL DIVERSITY in URBAN AMERICA

Wallace E. Lambert
and
Donald M. Taylor

 PRAEGER

New York
Westport, Connecticut
London

Library of Congress Cataloging-in-Publication Data

Lambert, Wallace E.
    Coping with cultural and racial diversity in urban America /
Wallace E. Lambert and Donald M. Taylor.
        p.   cm.
    Includes bibliographical references and index.
    ISBN 0-275-93174-9
    1. Ethnology—United States. 2. Pluralism (Social sciences)—
United States. 3. Acculturation—United States. 4. United States—
Ethnic relations. 5. United States—Race relations.   I. Taylor,
Donald M.   II. Title.
    E184.A1L25   1990
    305.8'00973—dc20   89-16097

Copyright © 1990 by Wallace E. Lambert and Donald M. Taylor

Library of Congress Catalog Card Number: 89-16097
ISBN: 0-275-93174-9

First published in 1990

Praeger Publishers, One Madison Avenue, New York, NY 10010
A division of Greenwood Press, Inc.

Printed in the United States of America

The paper used in this book complies with the
Permanent Paper Standard issued by the National
Information Standards Organization (Z39.48-1984).

10 9 8 7 6 5 4 3 2 1

Contents

Acknowledgments

Many people offered us the help necessary to make this investigation possible. First, we are especially grateful to the Spencer Foundation for their financial and personal support of the major aspects of the study, and to the Social Science and Humanities Research Council of Canada for financing local pretesting and student part-time help. Second, we want to thank Dr. Naomi Holobow, a research associate at McGill, who offered us continuous assistance with data analysis and interpretation. Third, we are indebted to four students at McGill for their discussions and interpretations of the findings: Geoffrey Hall, Lambros Mermigis, Gertie Witte, and Barbara Gasiorek. Fourth, we are extremely grateful to Clarence Pilatowitz, Elba Berlin, Marcia Nowakowski, Nicholas Prychitko, John Radwanski, and Maria Etienne, educators in the greater Detroit school systems, for their cooperation and support throughout the investigation. Fifth, we want to thank, most sincerely, Mrs. Minerva Kuhlenschmidt and Miss Im Ong for their care, patience, and good humor in typing numerous drafts of the text and tables. Finally, it was extremely valuable for us to have former Prime Minister Pierre Elliott Trudeau take the time to read an early draft of our study and then arrange to spend a morning with us and our students discussing the interpretations and implications of our findings.

COPING WITH CULTURAL
and RACIAL DIVERSITY
in URBAN AMERICA

1

The American Challenge:
Assimilation or Multiculturalism

The "American persona" has been recently described in terms
of three national preoccupations, namely, concerns about
war and peace, about bread and butter, and about black and
white. Interesting as this overview is, we feel it misses
what may be the most distinctive feature of all: a
preoccupation and underlying concern in the United States
with what is or is not "American." The research described
in this monograph deals indirectly with this deeply rooted
American concern. However, the label "American" is really
an imprecise misnomer. Mexicans and Canadians are also
Americans in the technical sense. We will use the term
nonetheless because, for residents of the United States,
being "American" or "an American" is the popular and common
label.
   The research to be described is a community based
investigation of the attitudes of Americans--some
mainstream, long-term residents and others who are first or
second generation immigrants--towards ethnic diversity and
intergroup relations. An underlying theme to the research
is: How far can an ethnic group in the United States go in
maintaining its identity before that group trespasses into

a "that's un-American" terrain? In this sense, our study deals with cultural diversity and "multiculturalism" on the one hand and on the other hand with "assimilation". It is therefore a study of "E pluribus unum" and the question of how it is possible to protect the "unum" if the "pluribuses" become too numerous and too distinctive.

The study was conducted in a metropolitan area in the United States which, like many others, is constantly accommodating to the social pressures generated by daily contacts between and among members of a large array of ethnic groups, some visible "minorities" and others hardly visible at all. Because of their ethnicity, the groups in question might in some instances be seen as minority groups, and in other cases as immigrants, neo-Americans, or simply hyphenated Americans. However, in their own minds, many of these people don't think of themselves as any less "American" than anyone else. Many are puzzled by what it means to be "American" and by the social forces exerted on them to become more "American" than they are. Thus, the main characters in this story are working-class adults living in a major urban center, some of whom are established mainstreamers while others are newcomers, but all of whom experience ethnic and racial diversity as a constant, palpable, daily fact of life.

Controversies about multiculturalism versus assimilation impinge on nearly every aspect of social life in the United States. Setting aside daily interpersonal encounters with ethnic diversity, debates and contrasting views about the underlying issues find their way regularly into the media, and into local and national policies on education, employment, and civil rights in general. The same debates are rekindled and revised as changes in the demographic structure of the nation take place. The controversies become particularly intense when choices have to be made among political candidates, when "equal opportunity" rules are applied in community relations or in housing, or when school committees decide on the use of languages other than English for schooling. As one would expect, the same basic controversies emerge in the theoretical and empirical work of scholars who have made the study of assimilation and multiculturalism their full-time preoccupations. Here we will elaborate briefly on each of these manifestations of this fundamental American debate.

MULTICULTURALISM AND ASSIMILATION: CONTROVERSY IN THE PRINT MEDIA

The underlying concerns Americans have about what is or isn't American seep through the opinions and attitudes reported daily in news and editorial items. In fact, one could construct an instructive social history of the nation by systematically collating such opinions and attitudes. Consider the following haphazard sample of news items and editorials.   Later we'll compare these with comparable reports in an earlier phase of America's history. In both instances, we find clear examples of struggles among ethnic groups, symptoms of ethnic group growth and mobilization, and the consequences, both negative and at times sympathetic, such changes engender.

Headline: **President Assailed on School Bill Veto**

Civil rights advocates and Chicago school officials have denounced the presidential veto of a bill that would have provided $20 million to help desegregate Chicago's public schools... Of the 435,000 students in Chicago's public schools, Mr. Howard (of the Chicago Board of Education) said, 61 percent are black, 20 percent are Hispanic, 16 percent are white and 3 percent are Asian. Officials said black and Hispanic children accounted for 90 percent of the enrollment in the schools that would have received aid... The Administration has cited Chicago's desegregation plan as a model of how to integrate urban schools without mandatory busing. But it has opposed court orders to help bring about desegregation by financing the upgrading of education in black and Hispanic neighborhoods (International Herald Tribune, August 16, 1983).

Headline: **Latinos Charge Administration Ignores Them**

Four national Latino organizations have attacked the administration on issues ranging from jobs to foreign policy, charging that the president has misrepresented his record on issues affecting Hispanic Americans... 'This president has done very little to address the problems of Hispanics', Arnold Torres, of the Latin American Citizens, said...'I guess we're third in line'. He scoffed at Mr. Reagan's statement to a Mexican American audience in El Paso that he had served enchiladas to Queen Elizabeth of Britain when she visited his ranch. 'That was not a joke', Mr. Torres said. 'Hispanics want more than to know what's on the menu' (International Herald Tribune, August 26, 1983).

Headline: **Experts Plan to Address Ills of Black Family**

Black leaders and others are to meet next year to fashion a comprehensive program addressing the problems of black American families, the National Association for the Advancement of Colored People announced yesterday... The association provided statistics to show that households headed by black women have a median income about a third of that for all American families and that single women, many of them teenagers, are giving birth to more than half of the black babies born in the United States... Benjamin L. Hooks, executive director of the N.A.A.C.P., said in a statement that 'finding ways to end the precipitous slide of the black family is one of the most important items on the civil rights agenda today... If the child returns home to a family devoid of the basic tenets necessary for his discipline, growth and development, the integrated school environment must fail' (New York Times, September 13, 1983).

Headline: **Asian-Americans See Growing Bias**

Asian-American leaders say they are alarmed by what they regard as rising discrimination against their people. As a result, they are forming political action organizations around the country that are unifying traditionally rival ethnic groups, including Japanese, Koreans, Chinese and Vietnamese... 'It's come to the point that as long as you 'look' Asian, you're open to attack, regardless of which group you belong to', said

Stewart Kwoh, director of the Asian Pacific Legal
Center...   'The only road open for us is to get
active politically, by unifying all the Asians to
form a viable force, so when we speak, we speak in
one voice', said Lin Chung...   The rising tension
between Asians and blacks was reflected this month in
The Los Angeles Sentinel which calls itself the
largest black-owned newspaper in the West.   In a
blunt, four-part series, the newspaper reported that
scores of businesses in black areas had recently been
'taken over' by Asians...   'It is usually other
minority groups who resent Koreans and give trouble
to them', said Dong Soo Ha, of the Korean Association
of New York.   'Some are Hispanics, some black, some
Haitians, it depends on the neighborhood.'...   'A lot
of the Anglo parents think these kids are slowing
down classes', said Betty Waki, a Japanese American
high school teacher.   Some parents have complained
that the inability of many Asian children to speak
English has required bilingual teaching programs that
they say impede the progress of other children
(New York Times, September 10, 1983).

Headline: **Quixotic Sentencing**

Two nights before he was to be married, Vincent
Chin and three friends went out to celebrate in a
Detroit bar. During the course of the evening, a
fight broke out between Mr. Chin and his friends and
two white men.   An eyewitness said that Mr. Chin, a
Chinese American, was mistaken for a Japanese, and
that hard times in the Motor City have increased
racial animosity toward Asians in general.   But
whatever the cause of the dispute, no one denies that
Mr. Chin was beaten to death with a baseball bat by
the two white men (New York Times, May 6, 1983).

Headline: **A Young Black Man Asks: Will I Be Next?**

Another young African American man has fallen
victim to the bullets of prejudice and hatred. Yusuf
Hawkins, 16 years old, minding his own business, was
shot to death on a New York City sidewalk last week
by a gang of white kids.

I am writing this in the middle of the night, unable to sleep. I wonder if I am to be next... I cannot walk throughout the city in which I was born without fearing for my safety--just because I am an African American... Why is this happening to me in my own beloved country? Do white people secretly aspire to intern us all in jails or concentration camps--to permanently do away with us?... I certainly am shouldering my share of these responsibilities that accompany the privileges of American citizenship. Moreover, I and all other Americans have something positive and meaningful to contribute to this country. Therefore, I must state that I will not appease those of you who wish me dead... Those murderers among you better realize that, because I am an American, I will defend myself...

This latest killing of an innocent, unarmed young black man gives me the feeling of impending doom. I hope that I am overreacting, but unfortunately for me, as well as other Americans, I doubt it (Devin S. Standard, New York Times, September 2, 1989).

Headline: **Arab-Bashing in America**

Ali Kamal Dakroub, who fled the terrorism of Beirut in 1976, now watches his sons fend off local youths and endure the taunts of "camel jockey" and "rag head". Dearborn's estimated 20,000 Arab Americans have grown accustomed to increasing death threats, hate mail and vandalism, especially following the 1980 Iranian hostage crisis--even though Iranians are not Arabs. And the animosity grows with each new terrorist outrage overseas (Newsweek, January 20, 1986).

Headline: **Si Quiere Promover English**

The trouble with much 'bilingual' education is that it isn't bilingual. Too often it's a program to teach children math, social studies and science in their native language without any genuine effort to help them function in English as soon as possible. That moving children into English instruction is desirable should be beyond debate. Whatever the

transitional value of teaching them in a native
language, English is the essential skill for anyone
expecting opportunity in the United States.
'Bilingual' programs are worthy of Federal subsidy
only so long as achievement in English is their true
aim... Far from eliminating bilingual programs, as
its critics charge, the bill (submitted to Congress)
would make proficiency in English a primary
requirement for bilingual teachers, refine the
requirements for evaluating bilingual programs, and
let school districts decide whether their non-English
speakers are best served by 'immersion' (in English)
courses or transitional training in native languages.
For those who honestly hope to promote learning in
English, that seems the wisest course
(New York Times, September 13, 1983).

It is of interest that the same day in a separate
section of the same newspaper, the value of "immersion in
foreign languages" for English-speaking American children
was forcefully advocated, as seen in the next excerpt.

Headline: **Foreign Languages in Primary School**

In its 1979 report, the (President's Commission
on Foreign Language and International Studies)
declared that 'our gross national inadequacy in
foreign language skills has become a serious and
growing liability' that undermines the ability of the
United States to communicate and compete economically
with other nations... 'Learning to speak another
language is important because we live in a polyglot
society' said Frank C. Arricale, superintendent (of
District 19 in Brooklyn). 'There are also practical
reasons to have a second language. The bilingual
secretary or the bilingual truck driver will get more
money than the monolingual one' (New York Times,
September 13, 1983).

Headline: **One Nation, One Language for All**

Our society has enough divisive forces already;
language differentiation should not be another...

Our money is well invested in a program that helps our immigrants become American (Nation's Business, December 1980).

Headline: **Carl Schurz's Legacy**

In an age when ethnic politics has become so controversial, it is well to remember that appeals from political leaders to immigrant interests are nothing new. In this tricentennial of German settlement in America, Carl Schurz, one of the greatest German Americans, deserves to be recalled as a model for ethnic politicians... Schurz's greatest contribution, however, was as immigrant leader. A model for his fellow Germans, he showed them that they could attain some of the highest distinctions in their new country. He also helped them cope with the problems of immigration--the culture gap, the new language and the strange customs. Learn English, he told them, but don't forget your mother tongue. Trying to fuse the best that was German with the best that was American, he believed that integration and the retention of ethnic traditions was the answer to the immigration problem. He spoke German at home, wrote the first volume of his reminiscences in German and the other two in English, and proudly said in Congress, 'Those who would meanly and coldly forget their old mother could not be expected to be faithful to their young bride' (New York Times, October 8, 1983).

Headline: **English Spoken Here, but Unofficially**

Three states will soon vote on proposals to make English their official language. It's a popular, bad idea. Few Americans dispute the importance of a common tongue; an open society thrives on open communication, and economic opportunity in America depends on knowing English. But to require it smacks of discrimination....

A group called U.S. English leads the official-English campaign. It insists that its sole aim is integration, not discrimination. But a newly disclosed 1986 memo by its chairman, John Tanton, has caused an uproar.   The group's president, Linda Chavez, resigned in protest this month and Mr. Tanton quickly quit, too....

The ballot questions in Arizona, Colorado and Florida have more to do with symbolism than reality. Advocates want a barricade against the emergence of a two-culture America.   Opponents see it as an affront to minorities.   English is, and should be America's language.   All who would live here should learn it. The overwhelming majority do, but America's traditions are stained by offensive laws that say they must (New York Times, October 29, 1988).

Headline: **College Head Asks Study of Spanish Be Required**

The president of Temple University, situated in a black and Hispanic neighborhood in north Philadelphia, wants to make Spanish a requirement for graduation by 1990...Such a requirement would help create a generation with an understanding and respect for the cultures of others and ease the problems of minority groups, he said (New York Times, January 18, 1986).

There are sentiments expressed in these reports that could bother mainstream Americans: the possibility that newcomers to the States and long-standing minority groups may never fully lose their distinctive cultural styles, that assimilation may never keep pace with ethnic diversity.   They could be bothered, too, by the possibility that some groups may never want to assimilate and that certain groups of newcomers, especially those that flaunt their ethnicity, may be simply residing and working in the United States but keeping their hearts elsewhere. Basically, there are grounds for concern about the power of multiculturalism.   What do minorities really want and what do mainstreamers think they want?

MULTICULTURALISM AND ASSIMILATION: POLICY IMPLICATIONS

The term "multiculturalism" is used in several ways. As a descriptive term, it refers to ethnic pluralism or the coexistence of distinctive ethnic, racial, or cultural subgroups in a society.   In a multicultural society, ethnic diversity and distinctiveness are apparent and at least some members of each group are presumed to be interested in maintaining a cultural identity. Multiculturalism is also a descriptive term for an ideology about ethnic diversity.   In any society, a subgroup of pro-multiculturalists will regard the maintenance of cultural heritages favorably; its promotion is considered good for the society as a whole.   Assimilationists are against the encouragement of ethnic diversity because it is seen as a divisive force, a threat to societal unity. Thus, some people will think of multiculturalism as the polar opposite of cultural cohesiveness and unity, making multiculturalism an ideological extreme, a form of pluralistic anarchy, lying at the "bad" end of a good-bad dimension.   However, for those who see social and national value in ethnic/cultural diversity, multiculturalism is seen as an ideal.

For some nations, and Canada is a prime example, multiculturalism is not only a term used to describe a national policy, but it has become a national objective. The Canadian "policy of multiculturalism" was pronounced by former Prime Minister Trudeau in the Canadian House of Commons in 1971.   This policy grew out of the recommendations of a governmental inquiry into tensions between ethnic and language groups in Canada in the late 1960s (The Royal Commission on Bilingualism and Biculturalism) which concluded in favor of supporting the maintenance of the ethnic identities of all groups.   To justify their position, the authors of the Commission report cited psychological reasons   (e.g., that people cannot be cut off from their cultural roots without psychological harm) as well as national reasons (e.g., that each thriving culture is part of a nation's valuable personal resources).   Canada has not always endorsed such an open, noble policy (see Berry, Kalin, & Taylor, 1977, Chap.1), but the fact that since the 1970s multiculturalism has become a Canadian national policy, and that since 1988 it has become an act of parliament with its own governmental ministry, indicates how one nation has taken a clear position on this universal debate.   In Canada, therefore, the government has made multiculturalism a policy as well as an ideal. In the thinking of Milton Gordon (1981), this means that Canada has moved toward a "corporate pluralism" (in contrast to "liberal pluralism") in that it formally recognizes racial and ethnic entities, gives them "formal standing as groups in the national polity", and recognizes "group membership as an important factor" in the distribution of political power and economic reward (Gordon, 1981, p. 183). Canadians are nonetheless as deeply involved in the same debates as are Americans, and it would be unfair to suggest, through invidious comparisons, that one nation has its "act" better together. There are signs that Canada may have similar degrees of intergroup tensions involving immigrants and minorities. For instance, at the policy level, Amiel (1984) indicates that many policy makers in Canada publicly applaud multiculturalism but in private interviews "state that Canada's official multiculturalism is a divisive and negative approach to social harmony" (1984, p. 7). At the community level, one encounters reviews like the following:

Headline: **Not Our Kind of People**

Much of the resistance to immigration is also based on a fear of eroding the country's traditionally white, Anglo-French culture. 'There is a strong undercurrent of racism in Canada', says an official at the Ministry of Employment and Immigration. Last year immigrants from Asia, Africa, and the Caribbean accounted for about half of new arrivals. Canadian society's changing complexion can be seen in Ottawa, where many cabs are driven by Pakistanis, or on the streets of Toronto, where a high proportion of newspaper stands are manned by Sikhs. 'I don't have anything against these people,' says a visitor to Toronto, John MacPherson, 54, a Manitoba farmer who wears a tartan necktie and a Scottish cap. 'But', he says, gesturing toward a turbanned Sikh, 'they're just not our kind of people....'
In a study for the government released two months ago...most of those interviewed...were opposed to Canada becoming a multicultural society (Time Magazine, February 3, 1986).

Other nations take contrasting stands, ranging from a rigid policy of   ethnic group segregation as in South Africa, to an ideal of forging one group   from the many that comprise the United States of America.   In each country,   regardless of policy, the debate pro and con multiculturalism is never   finally settled, and there are pressures today that make this debate again of   vital importance for all nations. And nowhere are the social and political issues as clear and discernible as they are in the United States.

Multiculturalism is a descriptive fact about the United States. The important issue of debate is the social policy of multiculturalism,   whether the traditional American policy of assimilation is adequate in the late twentieth century. Decision makers are being forced by circumstances to reevaluate the current policy and to reconsider various alternatives.   If a close and sympathetic neighbor like Canada has rejected a policy of melting-pot assimilation for one of multiculturalism based on an ethnic mosaic, perhaps there is a lesson to be learned from across the border? In any case, the Canadian stance brings the debate into sharper focus.

There is, however, a healthy, widespread skepticism in the United States about ethnically and linguistically pluralistic societies, an underlying fear that such nations can never be cohesive, that they are intrinsically divisive. The United States has shown that it can manage diversity of national origin and religion, and they are trying to learn to live with differences of skin color, but the idea of supporting language diversity has become staggering to contemplate. Can any society, the argument goes, be really unified if minority groups maintain their heritage languages? That question has had a spirited history in the United States (c.f. Grittner, 1987), and it seems that instruction through languages other than English is worrisome unless it is limited to private or community run schools.   It is difficult for most Americans to understand why it should ever take place in public schools. Tolerant as English-speaking Americans are of transitional bilingual education programs, the idea of maintaining heritage cultures and/or languages in public schools and institutions is unquestionably a worrisome, socially divisive, un-American alternative for the majority.

At the same time, there are others who challenge the majority view. David Hamburg, in his annual report as President of the Carnegie Corporation of New York, is well aware of the need for American self analysis:

> The underlying orientation of importance here is the ubiquitous human tendency toward egocentricism and ethnocentrism. We find it easy to put ourselves at the center of the universe, attaching a strong positive value to ourselves and our group, while attaching a negative value to many other people and their groups. It is prudent to assume that human beings are all, to some extent, egocentric and ethnocentric. But these tendencies, under certain conditions, can lead to violent conflict.
> No longer have we the luxury to indulge in prejudice and in ethnocentric extremes. These are anachronisms grounded in our ancient past. There may be 'tough-minded' people who believe that this is the human condition and that we must make the most of it. But technology has passed them by. The destructive capacity of modern weapons—large and small, nuclear and non-nuclear—has made the 'tough-minded' view unrealistic, if not today, then tomorrow. If we cannot learn to accommodate each other respectfully—within nations and across nations—we will destroy each other at such a rate that humanity will soon have little to cherish, assuming there is any humanity left on earth (Hamburg, 1985).

This perceptive essay, written by an American concerned about intergroup conflict in the United States and elsewhere, is relevant to the present study because it explores the relation between basic human attitudes, like ethnocentrism and egocentrism, and their relation, in turn, to multiculturalism and assimilation as policies and ideals.

MULTICULTURALISM AND ASSIMILATION: DEMOGRAPHIC REALITIES

These differences of points of view from political community leaders are important indicators of the significance of the issues involved. There is more to the arguments and counter arguments than mere political Ping-Pong, for they are played out in real life social interactions in most American communities. Some people may enter such interactions with a socially divisive type of thinking about ethnic minorities, for instance, that minorities may be grateful for the opportunity to be in the United States, but because of their strong desires to maintain heritage cultures and languages, they may be much less interested in becoming American in the process. Coming from long-term residents, a perception of this sort about immigrant minorities could easily be interpreted as an expression of an ungrateful attitude and as an implied insult to the host community itself. There are of course other ways to interpret an ethnic group's strong desire to keep a heritage culture and language alive. These desires could be signs of a new form of internationalism that incorporates a perception of the world as shrinking in size and forcing a new type of interdependency among peoples who cohabit the world, coupled with a new conception of the attachments people make, not only to their "own" particular corners of the world, but to the world as a whole. However such perceptions arise and whatever interpretations are made of them, we as researchers are very much aware of the implications the various findings we will present in this study might have on intergroup harmony in most communities in the United States.

An important underlying factor that affects the debate and its resolution is the demographic makeup of the nation. There are fundamental demographic changes underway in the United States, changes that long-term residents may not recognize as clearly as newcomers to the United States do. It is no longer easy to describe what it is to be "American" or what the "American way of life" actually is. The United States has become a very ethnically diversified nation with surprisingly large ethnic subgroupings. According to Sowell (1983), only 14 percent of the total population of the United States have an Anglo-Saxon heritage, placing them on an equal numerical footing with those of Germanic heritage (13 percent), which is only slightly more than those with Afro-American roots (12 percent), or of Hispanic American ancestry (11 percent), with the likelihood of the latter group becoming the most numerous of all within the century. This diversification can have two quite different effects on ethnic minorities, especially immigrant or refugee newcomers. While it can confuse them about what they are expected to do to become more "American", it can also make their adjustment to the nation easier because by maintaining their ethnic identity, they can be as American as anyone else. Stated otherwise, by not rushing to become "Americanized", they thereby

become   progressively more like a large majority of other
equally ethnic Americans.   Thus, the demographic realities
of the nation prompt each member of an ethnic minority
group to confront a personal debate around the issue of
multiculturalism as an ideal and a policy.   Each has to
decide whether or not he/she is able to juggle a heritage
culture and language, along with a national culture and
language, and if it is worthwhile to do so.

MULTICULTURALISM AND ASSIMILATION: THEIR MANIFESTATION IN THE LANGUAGE ISSUE

The implications of any decisions about an appropriate
policy for dealing with cultural diversity are far
reaching, but nowhere do they surface more dramatically
than in the field of education and especially education
related to language.   That language should be so central is
not surprising.   Language, after all, is the major symbol
system people have for communicating with one another.   But
the simple communication aspect of the symbol is probably
not as important as the fact that languages define the very
core of ethnic identity (see Giles, Taylor & Bourhis, 1977;
Taylor, Basili & Aboud, 1973; Taylor & Simard, 1975).
It follows that any policy dealing with cultural
diversity can't help but have a profound impact on
language, and through language, on communication and social
identity.   However individuals or groups of individuals
deal with language in the privacy of their homes or within
the confines of their own community, it in itself does not
have fundamental consequences for the society as a whole.
How language is handled within the nation's educational
institutions, however, strikes at the very core of American
values.   The classroom is where young people's values are
shaped, where the youth are prepared to compete in a modern
technological society and where all, hopefully, are
provided with an equal opportunity to at least embark on a
chosen career path with the chance to pursue it as far as
their talents and efforts will permit.
What then are the implications of the debate over
multiculturalism for education in the United States?   To
begin with, a serious conflict emerges for children
attending English medium schools if their home language is
not English.   How are such "English deficient" children to
be educated?   One way is to treat them as one would any
Anglophone student.   The rationale underlying such an

approach is that the United States is an English speaking country; fluent English is needed in order to get ahead; therefore children should be exposed to as much English as possible. Such a philosophy seems to make good sense, but, on reflection, it may neglect certain values and realities. First, minority language children are placed at an immediate disadvantage in curriculum content areas compared to Anglophone children; second, such children lose a fundamental feature of their own personal identities; third, they progressively lose skill in their vehicle for communicating with their family; fourth, they witness a symbolic disrespect of their heritage; and fifth, the nation itself dispenses with a valuable resource that could, if cultivated, counteract American insularity.

Another approach currently in vogue in the United States is a form of bilingual education that attempts to ease the transition of non-English speaking children into the conventional English curriculum. Proponents agree that: the child must ultimately function as any other child in English; it will take a while before children can be comfortable in an all English environment, and we don't want them to get behind in content subjects; therefore, we will have native speakers of the home language of the children give compensatory teaching in the native language to insure that the children will grasp key concepts and to insure that for part of each day they will be comfortable with a teacher who shares their ethnic heritage.

This approach also has its drawbacks. First, it defines children as in need of bilingual education on the basis of poor scores on standard English tests. This by itself is not serious, but in the process the child is labelled as "deficient". Then by being "pulled out" of the class for special teaching, the child is further categorized until ultimately the labels "deficient" and "special" are perceived as true. A second problem is the linguistic model provided for the child. Since the aim is to "mainstream" the child as quickly as possible, the teacher or the teacher's aid who speaks the child's heritage language only uses that language when the child needs assistance in understanding concepts. This often means that in such interchanges the child is exposed to nonstandard English or a less than ideal English model. In most cases, this approach fails to capitalize on that teacher's expertise in the heritage language. Finally, because these interchanges are symptoms of deficiency of some sort, the child once again experiences a threat to his or her ethnic identity.

A third approach begins with the assumption that learning via one, two, or even three languages need not place any undue burden on the child, nor detract from the major aim of education (i.e., the intellectual and social preparation of young people for a highly competitive technological society). This orientation was developed in a Canadian context where the challenge was to have Anglophone children become fluently bilingual (English/French) without any costs in terms of their native language skills (English) or content subjects such as science and mathematics. This was the orientation that prompted the research initiated at McGill University by Lambert and Tucker (1972) on "early immersion" schooling wherein English-speaking children, with no French language experience in their homes and little if any in their communities, entered public school kindergarten or grade 1 classes that were conducted by a monolingual French-speaking teacher. This "early immersion" or "home-to-school language-switch" program, as it was called, is kept exclusively French through grade 2 and only at grade 2 or 3 is English introduced, in the form of a language arts program, for one period a day. By grade 4 particular subject matters are taught in English (by a separate native English speaking teacher) so that by grades 5 and 6 some 60 percent of the instruction is in English.

The concept of immersion schooling was based on a very important and fundamental premise: that people learn a second language in much the same way as they learn their first, and that languages are best learned in an incidental fashion in a context where the person is socially stimulated to acquire the language and is exposed to it in its natural form.

The consistent findings from nearly 20 years of longitudinal research on children in immersion programs permit several conclusions that bear not only on the linguistic consequences of the programs but on their psychological and social consequences as well (Lambert, 1981): (1) Immersion pupils are taken along by monolingual teachers to a level of functional bilingualism that could not be duplicated in any other fashion short of living and being schooled in a foreign setting. Furthermore, pupils arrive at that level of competence (2) without detriment to home-language skill development (3) without falling behind in the all-important content areas of the curriculum, indicating that the incidental acquisition of French does not distract the students from learning new and complex ideas through French;   (4) without any form of mental confusion or loss of normal cognitive growth;   and (5)   without a loss of identity or appreciation for their own ethnicity.   Most important of all in the present context,   (6)   they also develop a deeper appreciation for French Canadians by having learned about them and their culture through their teachers and through their developing skill with the language of French Canadians (see Lambert, 1982).

What is exciting about this program, over and above its educational and cognitive impact, is that it opens children's minds to an otherwise foreign and possibly threatening out-group.   It also provides certain of them with sociopolitical insights that monolingual mainstreamers would likely never have.   For example, the immersion children come to realize that peaceful democratic coexistence among members of Canada's distinctive ethnolinguistic groups calls for something more than simply learning one another's language.   Having learned the other language well and having learned to appreciate the other cultural group, children with immersion experience, when compared to control children, realize that effective and peaceful coexistence depends upon something even more important--opportunities for both ethnic groups of young people to interact socially on an equitable basis.   This is a very sophisticated insight.

Thus, a new approach to the development of bilingual skills and bicultural knowledge is now available, and since it works as well in other parts of Canada where few if any French Canadians are encountered in social life, it, or some variation of it, might be expected to work equally well in the United States (see Genesee, 1984; Lambert, 1984).

Note, however, that immersion education through a foreign or second language was designed for the English-speaking Canadian and the English-speaking American mainstreamers--the segments of American society most secure in their ethnic and linguistic identity, but the ones most in need of knowledge about and sensitivity towards other ethnic and linguistic groups.   To the extent that mainstream children are sensitized to and educated in another language and culture, the better the chances are of developing a fairer, more equitable society.   The better too are the chances of improving the self-views of ethnolinguistic minority children who are heartened and complimented when they realize that mainstream children are making sincere gestures to learn about them, their language, and their ways of life (see Taylor, 1987).

We have referred to this process of developing bilingual and bicultural skills among English-speaking Canadians or American children as an "additive" form of bilingualism, implying that these children, with no fear of ethnic/linguistic erosion, can add one or more foreign languages to their accumulating skills, and profit immensely from the experience, cognitively, socially, and even economically. Most mainstream parents, incidentally, are aware of these advantages and are surprisingly eager and anxious to have their children enroll in immersion programs or variants thereof. They want something more for their children than the traditional foreign language programs that they followed a generation ago: programs that failed to develop either language competence or cultural sensitivity.

However, we draw a very sharp contrast between the "additive" form of bilingualism described above and the "subtractive" form which constitutes a totally different psychological and social reality, having different outcomes, different potential hazards, and different means-to-ends demands (see Lambert & Taylor, 1983). The hyphenated American child, like the French-Canadian, embarks on a "subtractive" bilingual route as soon as he/she enters a school where a high prestige, socially powerful, dominant language such as English is introduced as the exclusive language of instruction. Perceptive members of ethnolinguistic minority groups have good grounds for worry and concern about the steam-roller effect of a powerful dominant language; it can make foreign home languages and cultures seem "homely" through contrast, ghosts in the closet to be eradicated and suppressed. The effects of this subtractive aspect of bilingualism and biculturalism among Francophone university students in Quebec has been carefully studied by Taylor, Meynard, and Rheault (1977). Two findings from the research help illustrate our main point. First, it was found that feelings of threat to one's ethnic identity function as a negative motivation in the second-language learning process. Second, it turned out that those Francophones who were least fluent in English were those who felt their cultural identity to be most threatened.

But just as French is too precious to be subtracted from Canadian society, so too, it can be argued, are the many "foreign" languages and cultures extant in America too precious to be eradicated from that society. Even more potentionally devastating is the cognitive risk minority language children run when their basic conceptual language--the linguistic system that has been used to form and express thoughts and ideas from infancy on--is abruptly put aside and suppressed so as not to interfere with the new school language.

A major responsibility of educational policy makers then becomes one of transforming subtractive forms of bilingualism and biculturalism into additive ones for the benefit of both the ethnolinguistic minority groups involved as well as the mainstreamers. Community experiments that attempt to implement such transformations, although few in number so far, are yet underway. Basically these new experimental programs call for schooling to be conducted in the frequently neglected home language of the ethnolinguistic minority child, starting at kindergarten or grade 1. The programs continue until it is certain that the home language is strongly entrenched and that the children are rooted in and oriented toward their ethnic identity. The programs of course provide a concurrent strand of English language instruction (in the form of English as a second language or English immersion, with a separate teacher) for part of the day, but the dual-track program involving home language instruction is maintained for the first three or four years of primary education. Only then, it is argued, can a switch to a mainly English language program safely take place.

Richard Tucker (1980) evaluated a number of such community-based studies and came to the conclusion that there is

> a cumulative and positive impact of bilingual education on all youngsters when they are allowed to remain in bilingual programs for a period of time greater that two or three or even five years and when there is an active attempt to provide nurturance and sustenance of their mother tongue in addition to introducing teaching via the language of wider communication (Tucker, 1980, p. 6).

This then becomes a challenging alternative for America: to help salvage minority languages and cultures and to help develop a new generation of children who could be happy to be both American and Hispanic, Haitian, Polish,

Navajo, Arabic, or whatever.   But note the essential
ingredients of this plan: (1)   at the same time as the
needs of the ethnic minority child are being catered to,
the mainstream child is simultaneously developing skills in
and an appreciation for at least one of these other
languages and its associated culture; and (2)   no time is
taken from the all-important task of developing competence
in the critical content subjects that make up a solid and
demanding educational curriculum.

Clearly, ethnic identity and heritage language
maintenance are inseparably linked, and the technical
literature on potentially useful new approaches to
developing bilingual and bicultural skills are available.
In planning the present study, however, we wondered how
much of the technical information has trickled down to
working class families in America's urban centers.   How
much importance do ethnic minorities give to heritage
language maintenance, and how do their views on the topic
match with those of Anglophone mainstreamers?   And what is
being done by school authorities and by ethnic community
leaders with regard to the development of bilingualism for
ethnic and nonethnic youngsters?

ASSIMILATION AND MULTICULTURALISM: A THEORETICAL AND EMPIRICAL ISSUE

In the time period 1820 to 1920, 33 million immigrants
entered the United States.   Since then, quite
understandably, a great deal of thinking has been directed
to ethnic and cultural diversity by American historians and
social scientists.   There are two main reasons for this
preoccupation with multiculturalism: first, the violence
and social cleavage that characterized social life in this
period of history and, second, the concerns Americans had
about the nation surviving because of internal ethnic
fissures.   The recent (1980s) editorials presented earlier
in this chapter reflect the current salience of ethnicity,
intergroup competition, and the ever-present dangers of
violence.   It is useful to reexamine briefly an earlier
period of American history to appreciate the persistence of
these themes and to comprehend the social climate in which
the extremely influential "classical" theories about
multiculturalism and assimilation were promulgated.

Kolodny (1969) gives us an excellent overview of
intergroup tensions as they affected the working class in

this earlier period. In the 1940s, ethnic group relations were being described in cold war terms. Writing about New England, Jones (1944) concludes:

> The "old Americans" are now an outnumbered clan, grimly holding on to financial and social power where they can, yielding only to death and superior taxes. The social cleavage they have thus created is, of course, the New England tragedy...Finding they are not wanted, the "immigrants" have struck back by two characteristically American attacks: they have conquered at the polls and they are trying to conquer in the counting house. New England is therefore a house divided against itself (Jones, 1944, pp. 214-215).

Further up in New England in Vermont, Anderson (1938) registered a similar community division:

> Economic barriers running horizontally and religious and ethnic barriers running vertically divide the community into small patches and set the pattern of [Burlington's] social life (Anderson, 1938, p. 182).

In a survey of 450 residents in 1938, Anderson asked: "Of what nationality are your close friends?" and found that French-Canadian and Jewish residents were very loyal to their own ethnic groups, but, most surprising of all, 87 percent of the "old American" group had close friends exclusively with their own group members.

Many years of ethnic group tension predated these ethnic divisions of the 1930s and 1940s, and much of the earlier conflict revolved around work and economic competition. For instance in Pennsylvania in the 1870s, over 90 percent of the foreign born coal miners were English speaking, but by 1910, Slavs and Italians comprised 66 percent, creating a sharp contest for "industrial supremacy" (meaning dominance in obtaining jobs) between old and new immigrants who formed "two distinctly marked groups" (Warne, 1913). Thus, "old" and "new" became associated with ethnicity, and this further escalated antagonisms. For instance, the textile plants in Massachusetts experienced numerous clashes of ethnic groups of workers who were seen at various times as either strike breakers or as noble protesters. In a mill town in 1903, a strike was broken by manufacturers who held out and finally reopened their mills. Lahne (1944) reports:

> The Portuguese, Poles and Greeks, who had been listed
> as unskilled help only, had meanwhile advanced to
> better positions when they went back to work, while
> the more skilled workers stayed out, and when the
> unions terminated the strike, many of the positions
> of their members had been filled and the union
> members displaced (Lahne, 1944, p. 74).

Resentments ran deep, as Kolodny explains:

> The new immigrant worker was not simply an impersonal
> force with which the native worker had to contend.
> He was of flesh and blood, speaking a certain
> language, having specific customs, and eating certain
> foods.   He and the rest of his group were
> identifiable.   They became objects of resentment and
> a stereotype of the group was created.   Its members,
> according to the stereotype, were not only different,
> they were physically and morally dirty... ignorant...
> unsanitary (Kolodny, 1969, p. 17).

Immigrant and minority ethnic groups therefore were
psychologically as well as socially segregated, and in the
work force they could be used by employers against
organized labor unions.   Some, like the United Mine
Workers, stressed a program of recruiting ethnic minorities
while others, like the United Textile Workers, did not.
They tended rather to exclude new immigrants, and expressed
open hostility to labor organizations such as the
Amalgamated Textile Workers, which represented mainly
ethnic minorities, by calling them "un-American, Bolshevik
and Jewish" (Lahne, op. cit., p. 248).
Young, writing in the 1930s saw the economical and
social consequences of this hostility:

> Labor as a whole suffers from the exclusion of
> Negroes and other minorities from the benefits of
> union organization, but individual workers may for a
> time ride along in an impermanent security from
> minority competition.   It is this ever-present
> possibility of immediate gain which helps keep alive
> a belief in the value of racial solidarity even where
> economic forces may be shown to make it a detriment
> in mass competition (Young, 1932, p. 417).

The one underlying truth of these accounts of American history is the persistence up to the present of ethnic cleavages that influence the economics and the politics of life in America. As Danzig concluded:

> Wherever we look--whether in heavy industry or dairy farming, public utilities or banking, the building or the garment trades, organized crime or law enforcement--we find clearly marked ethnic patterns of occupational opportunities. Though these patterns may have been breaking down in recent decades, in many of the older industries and vocations it still makes a difference whether one's forebears came from Ireland or Italy or whether one's first name or last is Milton (Danzig, 1964, p. 43).

Coming up to the present, it still clearly "makes a difference". The cover résumé of a powerful new bestseller in the United States, T. Wolfe's The Bonfire of Vanities (1987), puts it this way:

> This is a book about the human comedy of New York in the last years of the twentieth century, a city boiling over with racial and ethnic hostilities and burning with the itch to Grab it Now (Wolfe, 1987, cover flap).

And it still "makes a difference" not only for adults, but for young people as well. As Kolodny put it:

> The Negro-white situation aside, ethnic tensions persist in America and ethnic awareness continues to play a prominent part in the self-perception of those who grow up in our country (Kolodny, 1969, p. 23).

But it is difficult to put "aside" the black-white situation, and it is not easy to argue that black-white tensions have "broken down" all that much through time.

THE DEVELOPMENT OF EXPLANATORY THEORIES

Social scientists wanted to know what was happening in this inherently wealthy new world nation that prided itself on the fact that all people are or were immigrants and that, as a nation, all who wanted to come were welcome.

The Classical Assimilation School of Thought

Park and Burgess writing in 1921 presented the classical view of what they believed was really happening. They argued that ethnic groups and minorities gradually "assimilate". The definition was:

a process of interpenetration and fusion in which persons and groups acquire the memories, sentiments and attitudes of other persons or groups, and by sharing their experience and history, are incorporated with them in a common cultural life (Park and Burgess, 1921, p. 735).

The assumption was that with time ethnic differences and rivalries would disappear. Even coming from distinguished scholars, this could be as much a wishful illusion as a reality, because perceptive observers were the first to realize that something had to give if the nation was to survive such numbers of newcomers. Assimilation, even if gradual, seemed like the only alternative available. It is not all illusion, of course, and although still not fully explained one can understand M.M. Gordon when he stated that this nation, largely white, Anglo-Saxon, and Protestant in its beginning, "has absorbed over 41 million immigrants and their descendants from variegated sources and welded them into the contemporary American "people" (Gordon, 1961, p. 263). We may still wonder, however, about the strength of the welding and about how long it takes to assimilate, or if it ever is a completed process.

American sociologists turned to Europe for ideas in their attempts to explain the developments in American society, (see Coser, Nock, Steffan, and Rhea, 1987). Three people were of major influence: Marx, Durkheim, and more recently, Myrdal. Karl Marx had held out hope for assimilation because he believed that in capitalist societies, workers would become more loyal to their occupational class than to their family, nationality, or community. Emile Durkheim, the French sociologist, also anticipated that ethnic or "folk" communities along with their traditions would be replaced by ties between co-workers and neighborhood groups who shared common interests. This was likely because industrialization intensifies the "division of labor" into highly specialized, tight subgroups. More recent sociological thought has been influenced, also in the direction of assimilation, by the work of Gunnar Myrdal, a Scandinavian scholar, who studied black-white relations in the United States (Myrdal, 1944). Myrdal believed that the cultural inconsistency or dissonance between the American belief that "all men are created equal" and the American tendency toward racial discrimination and prejudice would not hold up. White racism would ultimately give way and permit blacks to finally assimilate (see Coser et al., 1987).

American sociologists adapted and extended these theoretical ideas, coming from the old world, for the American scene. In 1914 an influential play in New York was entitled The Melting Pot in which the notion was developed that America was becoming a superior society because of a "fusion of all the races" (Zangwill, 1914), making diversity and ethnic amalgamation a positive, valued trait of the American character. Park's views were influenced by the melting pot idea. His "contact hypothesis" suggested that America's ethnic diversity would lead to assimilation and accommodation which would involve both the newcomers and the host groups (Park, 1928). Through industrialization, people would move from farms to cities where they would make contact with other peoples, compete with them for jobs, accommodate to one another and ultimately assimilate. Some would be temporarily caught between old and new cultural systems, the stage of "marginality" (Park, 1928), but with time and through generations, this too would evolve into assimilation. The belief was that interpersonal associations across ethnic groups is more powerful and durable than interpersonal competition (see also Warner and Srole, 1945).

The Pluralist School of Thought

An opposing point of view developed slowly but surely as other theorists began to ask questions about the time course of assimilation. Certain ethnic groups like American Jews seemed to stay Jewish at the same time as they became successful and "structurally assimilated at the highest professional levels" (Coser, et al., 1987). And black Americans, since the slave era, have certainly not been assimilated, as had been predicted.

The counter view to assimilation has been labeled the "pluralist" school of thought. Its proponents questioned the inevitability of assimilation and the supposition that most members of most ethnic groups actually want to assimilate, seeing the nation instead as a cultural "mosaic" (Greeley, 1974), with a developing new ethnicity, called a "common" culture, that is quite different from that of the original host group and different too from the heritage cultures of the newcomers (Yancey, Ericksen & Juliani, 1976). Thus, the assimilation idea may have been overstated (see Abramson, 1973; Glazer and Moynihan, 1970).

Milton Gordon, considered by some as a classical assimilation theorist and by others as a developer of the pluralism position, saw important relations between the opposing sets of ideas (Gordon, 1964). He distinguished various stages of assimilation: "cultural" assimilation, where ethnic minorities adopt the language, values, and habits of the receiving nation; "structural" assimilation where ethnic minorities enter in large numbers into established institutions; "marital" assimilation and finally "identificational" assimilation where ethnic groups change traditional allegiances and adopt a sense of peoplehood based on the host society. Thus Gordon viewed the nation as pluralistic because different ethnic groups at any point in time function at particular stages, and some don't seem to move at all. To Gordon, pluralism in America is "incomplete assimilation" (Coser et al, 1987).

A healthy debate has thus been generated among American scholars specializing in intergroup relations. Some current leaders see overstatements on both sides and thereby direct attention to the need for more detailed, informative research on the topic of assimilation and multiculturalism. For instance H.J. Gans (1962; 1979) rejects the idea that a real ethnic revival is currently taking place. What seems to be happening instead is that ethnic groups have become more visible as a result of their upward mobility or because they have fallen into an underclass and thus kept out of competition. Many members of ethnic groups then adopt a "symbolic ethnicity", a type of nostalgic regeneration of love and pride in the old country and its traditions that is felt but not incorporated into everyday behaviour. Gans perceives the trend towards assimilation as still powerful and dominant; only those aspects of ethnicity which can be transformed into symbols and which can be easily practiced will persist. Perhaps so, but could this also be an example of Americans seeing what they want to see? Where should we draw the line between symbolic assimilation and the real thing?

Extensions and Modifications of the Classical Theories

In the early 1960s, Nathan Glazer and Daniel Moynihan (1963) asked themselves a simple, straightforward question: Have ethnic minority groups in the United States actually assimilated?   In their thought-provoking study, they concluded that ethnic minorities had, to an unexpected extent, maintained their ethnic identification through successive generations.   In fact in 1983 the two authors looked back at their 1963 forecast and congratulated themselves on the accuracy of their earlier 1963 predictions--that no basic change in the trend toward ethnic maintenance would take place in the succeeding twenty year period (Perlez, 1983). This general outcome, however, has prompted a very lively debate that is still in progress about the actual depth of ethnic maintenance in the United States.   In contrast to Glazer and Moynihan, Richard Alba, working with the 1980 census data, sees clear signs of progressive assimilation.   Focusing on intermarriage statistics, he finds increasingly large proportions of Americans with European heritages marrying outside their ethnic groups (see Collins, 1985).   It should be noted though that these marriage choices appear to be closely bound by social class and color lines.   Thus, Americans of Italian, Portuguese, Anglo-Saxon, and Jewish background tend to be intermarrying if they are of comparable social class standing, whereas blacks, whites, and most Asian groups overwhelmingly marry within ethnic boundaries, and presumably within social class boundaries as well.

Counter arguments in the debate take many forms (Collins, 1985; Isajiw, 1983). Does it necessarily follow that mixed ethnic marriages eradicate one or both of the contributing ethnic heritages? One study of the children of such unions found, in fact, that the adolescent offspring of mixed ethnic parents appreciated both sources of their own biethnicity, respected both parents and their backgrounds and showed strong signs of bilingualism in the languages involved (Aellen & Lambert, 1969). Thus, it could be that intermarriage permits family members to be "double-breeds" rather than "half-breeds" or "no-breeds". Working with the same 1980 census data, Moynihan (Collins, 1985), comes to a different conclusion than Alba. He notes that 83 percent of the American people in the 1980 census defined themselves in terms of their ethnic backgrounds; only 6 percent referred to themselves as

"Americans" or "from the U.S.A.".   Moynihan also suggests that there are twice as many ethnic parades in New York now than was the case twenty years ago, and many more ethnic language storefront signs in public view (Wolfe, 1985).
This important debate about how to interpret the present state of ethnic diversity in the United States will certainly continue and at each stage it provides us with new insights, even though we still have no complete answers to the basic questions.

Social psychologists have become interested in the debates and theory constructions about assimilation and multiculturalism because they believe that the underlying feelings and attitudes of those involved have not been adequately treated.   For instance, the multiculturalism alternative to assimilation suggests that successful social policies require a reduction in egocentric and ethnocentric thinking. Ethnocentric thinking is characterized by an emotional exaggeration of the value of one's own ethnic group relative to other groups.   A substantial number of research studies by social psychologists have shown that the more favorably one's own group is perceived, the less attractive other groups are viewed, making ethnocentrism one psychological mechanism that promotes ingroup-outgroup cleavage and prejudice of all forms (e.g., Levine & Campbell, 1972; Morse & Allport, 1952; Allport, 1954; Lambert & Klineberg, 1967; Jones & Lambert, 1959, 1965, 1967).   How might one reduce such negative thinking?   The Canadian multiculturalism policy was developed mainly as a means of avoiding the negative and divisive contrasts people make between and among ethnic groups that could be expected because of the "ubiquitous human tendency" toward ethnocentric thinking.   The assimilation argument eradicates the disruptive fallout of ethnocentric thinking on the part of various ethnic groups in a pluralistic society by trying, through melting-pot assimilation, to reduce sharp distinctive differences of ethnicity.   After all, the philosophy of assimilation emphasizes similarities and deemphasizes differences.   The counter argument, as presented by Prime Minister Trudeau in Ottawa in 1971, was to attenuate ethnocentrism by allowing and helping each ethnic group in a nation develop security, pride, and a sense of permanence in its ethnic identity. Ethnic security, it was believed, should promote intergroup respect and collaboration, permitting ethnic differences to flourish, thereby contributing to a broad national sense of unity through a diversified mosaic of ethnicities.   This

alternative clearly emphasizes differences, and in cases
where differences are significant to a group, the emphasis
might well be appreciated.

Underlying the political and social debate over
assimilation and multiculturalism are two fundamental
psychological processes. The assimilationist perspective
for example rests on the well established psychological
relationship between similarity and attraction. Laboratory
and field research converge on the fact that the more
people are similar to one another, the more they are
attracted to one another (e.g., Byrne, 1971; Newcomb,
1961). Indeed, Kandel (1978), has found that similarity in
terms of ethnic group membership is an important
determinant of friendship. The basic principle, then, is
entirely consistent with assimilation: minimizing ethnic
differences increases similarity, enhances the possibility
for attraction, and thereby reduces intergroup tensions.

However, multiculturalism as a policy is itself based
on the important psychological principle that openness to
novelty in the environment is increased to the extent that
the individual feels a sense of confidence and security.
In terms of multiculturalism then, it is precisely when a
person is secure in his or her own ethnic identity that
they can feel open and charitable towards others.
Eradicating ethnic differences from this perspective would
only threaten a person's sense of ethnic security and
thereby lead to intergroup tensions.

In fact, this hypothesis about multicultural thinking
has been tested by researchers in the Canadian setting.
Berry, Kalin, and Taylor (1977) conducted a large-scale
study among English and French speaking Canadians and found
partial support for the idea that the more secure and
comfortable group members were with their ethnic
identities, the more charitable and favorable they were
towards each other and towards other ethnic minority groups
in Canada (see also Jones & Lambert, 1959). This finding
suggests that there might be a viable alternative to
melting-pot assimilation and the similarity attraction
relationship upon which it is based. However, a recent
follow-up study poses some serious questions about the
multicultural alternative. That study focused on the
attitudes of one of the major "other" ethnic groups in
Canada--the Greek Canadians (Lambert, Mermigis, & Taylor,
1986), and found, as predicted, that the more Greek
Canadians were secure and comfortable with their ethnic
identity, the more favorable were their perceptions of

Anglophones and Francophones and other ethnic minorities, but this own-group security and pride did not promote a willingness to interact with other ethnic groups. Instead, the willingness to interact socially was determined more by a lack of ethnocentric thinking. Thus, the research to date partially supports the multicultural alternative, but it also partially supports an ethnocentrism alternative that has to be dealt with even when ethnic security is assured.

Again, we encounter an important debate this time at the level of theory and research. And this is much more than an academic debate. If one were to ignore the potential of multiculturalism, people could be robbed of a sense of their identity and this might serve to amplify social unrest and ethnic group frustrations. Similarly, one might jeopardize national unity and intergroup relations if one were to embrace a multiculturalism ideology and in practice it proved that similarity and attraction are actually causally related.

The Focus on Ethnic Group Competition in Current Theorizing

Recent extensions of the classic debate revolve around three concepts: "ethnic identity", "ethnic solidarity", and "ethnic mobilization". The descriptive labels used by today's scholars are revealing because they also are cold war terms; they reflect the concern of more established groups that recently arrived ethnic groups enter the American social system not only to compete but also to succeed. Highly motivated and resourceful newcomers pose a threat to American adults in the world of work, and to American youth who find themselves in schools with ethnic minority children who are dead serious about education and about learning how to advance in the new society.

In these recent formulations, competition plays a critical role in the descriptions given of intergroup relations between host members and immigrant or refugee newcomers to the host society. The claim is made that the classical accounts of the immigration process are inadequate because they have neglected the importance of ethnic group competition.

For example, a formerly accepted and "classical" view, presented by Hechter (1974, 1977), is that ethnic self-awareness and salience is a simple process that is activated when immigrant newcomers enter the host society and take up lower status and disadvantaged occupational and residential positions which segregate them into "ethnic enclosures" (see Portes, 1984), thereby creating a type of "internal colonialism" (Hechter, 1974; 1977).   If people enclosed in this way are either unable (or prevented) from entering and assimilating into the mainstream society, the ethnic features that characterize them as members of peripheral minority groups will be enhanced in their own thinking and in the thinking of others.   Thus, it might transpire that stereotypes develop about Puerto Ricans and Chicanos who cannot (or do not) advance any better than blacks in the United States, while Cubans, Poles, and Greeks do.

According to this view, if one were to give groups a chance to assimilate to American ways and to develop an American ethnic identity, ethnic solidarity and mobilization would recede.   According to the more recent "competition" theories (Nagel, 1982; Olzak, 1982; Portes, 1984), this isn't at all how group identities develop, nor is it how ethnic mobilization actually works.   Instead, it is argued, there is something much more "dynamic", adjustive, or "developmental" about ethnic awareness and saliency (Nagel & Olzak, 1982).   Several examples are given where ethnicity is changed or "converted" for very practical reasons.   In northern Nigeria, for instance, non-Hausa immigrants take on Hausa ethnicity when it is viewed as advantageous (Cohen, 1969), similar to non-Nubians conversions to Nubian ethnicity in Uganda (Kasfir, 1979), or changes made by minority groups to identify with dominant ethnic groups in the military in India, Peru, and Nigeria, as described by Enloe (1980).   Theoretically, then, ethnic identity would change back or reconvert if the situation called for it.   There are other less dramatic examples of flexibility throughout the world in the form of code switching and switches in bilingual identity in which case individuals temporarily or circumstantially take on one ethnic identity or another (see Angle, 1976; Lambert 1967).   Thus, ethnic identity is potentially fluid and adjustable, not necessarily tied to deep-seated, old country values which are automatically elicited in segregated, disadvantaged life experiences, or in intergroup contacts that highlight ethnic contrasts.

Nor does it follow that the strength of ethnic identity diminishes as newly arrived ethnic groups assimilate to the host society.   The gist of most recent

sociological thought runs just the opposite: as ethnic
minorities "start to abandon their internal colonies,
neighborhoods, and enclaves, and compete directly with
other groups, awareness of racial and cultural differences
will be heightened and form the basis of mobilization"
(Portes, 1984, p. 385, drawing on the work of Nagel, 1982;
Olzak, 1982; Nagel & Olzak, 1982).   The argument then is
that consciousness of ethnic contrasts is enhanced as group
members become more successful in the competition for
occupational and residential advancement.

These notions of "ethnic competition" and "ethnic
identity dynamism" have many proponents in the behavioral
sciences today.   The hypothesis is supported by a limited
number of empirical studies which show that those who have
assimilated or who can successfully assimilate (not the
unsuccessful, "colonized" members) are sometimes the very
ones who experience ethnic identity most clearly and who
champion ethnic mobilization movements.   Examples are seen
in the elites who direct the French Canadian separatist
movement in Quebec (Breton, 1978; Esman, 1987; Lambert,
1988), the Flemish movement in Belgium (Nielsen, 1986) and
the recent Cuban movement in Miami (Portes, 1984).

Taylor and McKirnan (1984) take the theory one step
further.   In terms of their five stage model of intergroup
relations they argue that group awareness and group
identity are promoted by group leaders who actively engage
in consciousness raising.   Group leaders, it is said, are
those who are unsuccessful in their attempts to be accepted
into mainstream positions of status.   These group leaders
who are turned away from mainstream status positions
attribute their failure to discrimination, and thereby
instigate consciousness raising among members of their own
ethnic group.

The Cuban example is particularly relevant to our own
investigation because it highlights the important roles
played by attitudes and social perceptions that each ethnic
group holds of themselves and of other groups (Portes,
1984).   Until the 1980s, the original anti-Castro Cuban
Americans had become extremely successful in terms of
occupational status, property and material possessions, and
in community power, especially in Florida.   They had
succeeded in competition, in the American fashion, and had
gained the respect of many host residents, along with the
resentment of those who were not as successful. In 1980,
the "Mariel" exodus occurred when Castro permitted (or
purposely sent) 125,000 new Cuban refugees to leave the

beach of Mariel and come to Florida. Shortly thereafter, a Gallop poll revealed that various samples of Americans placed Cubans at the bottom of a social distance scale in terms of desirability as possible neighbors. About the same time, and following in short order, a referendum was passed in Dade County, Florida that prohibited the use of any language other than English in education or cultural events.

These rapid-fire events prompted reactions from the established Cuban American population: a general shock and surprise about how they were evaluated by others; a pronounced increase in a sense of their identity; and a new surge of inter ethnic group competition directed by Cuban Americans, leading to the creation of four "important Cuban organizations concerned with domestic issues;" and finally, a surge of involvement of Cuban entrants into local politics and "power circles" (Portes, 1984). Portes sees these mobilization efforts as emanating especially from the younger, better-educated, and more assimilated Cuban Americans rather than from older members, less acculturated to America, and more restricted to ethnic enclaves.

This example is presented as support for the ethnic competition hypothesis and the relation of competition to ethnic identity and awareness. The basic argument is that:

> it is the breakdown of isolated ethnic communities, rather than their maintenance, which contributes decisively to the rise of ethnic awareness and mobilization. In the end, pressures of American urban life and the realities of increased competition have combined to transform a formerly isolated group into another ethnic minority, with goals and interests dependent on its position within American society (Portes, 1984, p. 395).

This interesting hypothesis about how ethnic identity, awareness, and mobilization are enhanced could be of great theoretical value. It provides us with a new slant on the process. But such ideas have to be tested on more than one group residing in one area of the United States, and the testing has to include carefully collected information about intergroup attitudes and perceptions which in the current formulations are simply assumed to play critical roles in the whole process. Nevertheless, this example of where current theory in the behavioral sciences is headed summarizes a number of research ideas that need to be carefully studied: Why are some ethnic and minority groups more prone than others to maintain a strong ethnic identity? How do parents' expectations for their children's educational and occupational futures differ for minority groups in comparison to established host resident groups? Why is the motivation to find or create work for family members so strong in particular ethnic groups and not in others? Does ethnic group success provoke resentment, envy, and aggression from other ethnic groups? Does it also sharpen ethnic identity boundaries?

Thus, the "assimilation" versus "multiculturalism" debate rages on many levels, from political and ideological to economic, social, and psychological. With so many, varied disciplines and perspectives contributing to the debate, there has arisen a need to return to the source of the issue: visible and nonvisible immigrants from varied cultural backgrounds who daily confront the problems of "getting ahead" in America. These are, to an important degree, the forgotten voices in the debate. Furthermore, the empirical data that shape current thought on the debate have neglected the attitudes and feelings of the main actors involved and concentrated instead on such factors as economic indicators, numerical trends in cross-cultural marriages, changes in government policy, the prevalence of ethnic newspapers, or the numbers and size of cultural parades and festivals.

Our aim in planning this study was to solicit the views and attitudes of representatives of all major groups involved in community intergroup relations. Rather than drawing inferences from secondary indicators of cultural attitudes, we wanted to present the debate about assimilation and multiculturalism squarely to the people involved, and to ask them directly where they stand on the debate and why. To complement and make sense of the views of immigrant ethnic newcomers to America it was necessary to include in our study "mainstream" Americans, both black and white, because they certainly are as involved with this debate as anyone else.

2

Methodological Approach

As the planning of the present study got underway, it was clear to us that there were at least two conflicting evaluations and interpretations of each of the key issues to be dealt with (i.e., multiculturalism, cultural diversity, "appropriate" behavior for immigrants and other minority groups, ways to safeguard national unity, and ways to reduce intergroup hostilities). Although no final answers are available for any of the theoretical debates involved, the debates are so socially important that systematic research seemed to us to be the mandatory next step.

Our basic aim was to solicit views on these key issues from a diverse array of American ethnic groups, all living in one urban center, and to do so in such a way that we could then construct a composite sketch of the underlying network of feelings, attitudes and beliefs that permeate life in multicultural settings in the United States. This of course is a very tall order. We wanted in particular the views of a large silent majority who are not usually surveyed--adults in the community who are of lower working-class backgrounds and whose ethnicity is obvious. With that as a base, their views could then be compared with those of more established mainstream whites and blacks, some from the same working-class backgrounds and neighborhoods, and others from more privileged socioeconomic backgrounds.

To assess the stand each ethnic group member takes on the debate about multiculturalism versus assimilation, we had to design the questioning so that both sides of each aspect of the debate would be presented for consideration. With this purpose in mind and after a series of pretests, the final interview schedule included as balanced a set of pros and cons on each topic as we could devise.   For instance, each respondent would be asked to evaluate the pros and then the cons that follow when members of ethnic groups give up their traditional ways: that by doing so, it would provide a common base for intergroup understanding (the pro side) versus the opposite view, that doing so would take away important features of ethnic and personal identity (the con side).   Similarly, each participant would evaluate the consequences of ethnic groups "maintaining" their traditional ways.   Would this tend to divide the nation into separate subgroups (the con side) or would it help each group feel secure in its group identity (the pro side)?   In this fashion, our final interview schedule permitted us to explore more extensively the thinking of members of various ethnic groups on a wide array of issues related to multiculturalism and to assimilation.   It was our contention that this type of pro/con probing would help us discern not only culturally distinctive perspectives of particular minority and majority groups, but also cross-cultural similarities in points of view.

Because the working-class adults we were to focus on were members of families, and because we were to deal with the issue of heritage language maintenance in public education, we chose to reach our adults through the public schools.   In fact, after two years of visiting the target area to conduct the research, we came to realize that, other than the innercity sidewalks, the public school is the only place where interethnic social contacts take place. Cross-group contacts are minimal or extremely rare in ethnic group gathering places such as a Polish bakery, a Mexican American restaurant, an Albanian sandwich shop, an Arab community center, or a black church, and they are also rare in any particular neighborhood.

Within the public schools, we could have chosen various groups of respondents as the focus for our study (e.g., an ethnically diverse group of children in public schools, teachers in multiethnic schools, or educators who set the policies for public schools).   Instead, we concentrated our efforts on ethnically distinctive parents with children in public schools.   Our reasoning was that

this was also a forgotten group in debates over public
education. Most research on education is in fact conducted
on school children, teachers, or administrators, and there
are not only sound research reasons for this, but pragmatic
ones as well. First and foremost, these popular targets of
research are easily accessible. Questionnaire and opinion
surveys can be conveniently conducted within the school
environment with such groups.   Second, these groups are
accustomed to dealing with research instruments and are
sufficiently familiar with formal education to make
gathering data streamlined and efficient. Thus it was with
some apprehension that we chose to deal with parents, the
most difficult group of all to survey. However, parents
obviously have a profound impact on children's values and
it is precisely these values that children bring to the
school environment.   In short, we based our study on
parents because parental views are a constant and powerful
source of influence on the child, especially when the
family environment can't help but strongly reflect the
heritage culture of the family.
    There are, of course, compelling reasons why parents
as a group have been so understudied, and we mention a
number of these reasons because they help place the present
study in context. The first problem is that, except,
perhaps, for occasional meetings at upper or middle-class
schools, parents simply do not attend school meetings and
functions.   This lack of attendance is an even bigger
problem in working-class communities where unemployment is
high and where the community is made up of newcomers to
America whose native language is not English. The result,
from a methodological perspective, is that parents must be
interviewed in their own homes which presupposes that
sufficient rapport can be established with members of each
community so that parents will agree to home interviews.
    A second problem is that a study of multiethnic
communities requires the use of a variety of languages
other than English.   This calls for care in complex
translations of research instruments.   As well,
interviewers must be fluent speakers of the language of the
respondent, and at the same time not biased in terms of
their own reactions to the questions asked.
    The multilingual problem is compounded by the fact
that the education of the parents is often very limited,
and indeed literacy itself may be a question. This is not
to suggest that the parents do not have well thought out
views on matters dealing with culture and language, nor

that they are any less interested in the educational experiences of their children. The problem lies more with social scientists who are purists and insist on formal settings, time-locked questionnaires, and standardized procedures. Our point here is that such demands would be artificial and, in the present case, impossible to uphold.

The final challenge was to adapt social psychological scaling procedures for use in a multilingual community and an interview context. Specifically, we wanted to avoid open ended questions that leave interpretation too much in the hands of researchers, or categorical yes/no answers that do not give respondents opportunities to express subtleties or shades of opinion. Thus, we wanted our respondents to answer according to a standard rating scale so that shades of opinion could be expressed and so that the data could be analyzed by means of sophisticated statistical procedures.

Briefly then, this study focuses on parents and their families living in a multiethnic and multilingual neighborhood. With one exception, the parent groups are all from working-class socioeconomic backgrounds. Our overall aim was to record in a standardized manner their views on the various debates involving assimilation and multiculturalism and the role of language in the debates. At the same time, we explored the implications of the debates for intergroup relations in the community and the role parents see for public schools in the entire process of bringing up their children in America.

THE RESEARCH SETTING

There were many possible research sites we could have chosen to conduct our survey. Indeed, any major metropolitan center in the United States is highly diverse in terms of ethnic, racial, and linguistic subgroups. We chose Detroit, Michigan as our research site because we had learned much about the city through a McGill-Detroit exchange program that dealt with problems of minority groups. Detroit is a challenging place to start this type of research. It is a large urban center that is in the process of accommodating, adjusting to, and learning from the nation's escalating ethnic and linguistic pluralization. Whatever we might discover in Detroit, we reasoned, should give us some good leads on what was going on elsewhere, even though the ethnic groups involved might be different. At least a Detroit-based study would provide us with a model and procedure for comparing various sites in the United States and elsewhere.

Hamtramck

On our first research visits to Detroit, specifically to Hamtramck, Michigan, we were cordially welcomed to visit schools, meet with parents, and talk with leaders of the major ethnic subcommunities.   There would be no trouble finding ample numbers of working class parents; the majority of ethnic group families met our major criterion: eligibility for free lunches at school because of economic hardships at home.   And the diversity of ethnic groups, some visible minorities, others not visible, was certain. There were sizable numbers of Polish American, black, Arab American and Albanian American families represented at all levels of the school population. However, there were "not any" Hispanic Americans in the community, nor could the staff or administrators think of any Anglo-American white families living in Hamtramck.   (The joke was that if we meant by "Americans of Anglo-Saxon heritage" what the community referred to as "American cowboys", then Hamtramck had none to offer!)   Nearby suburbs, especially Pontiac, Michigan, were suggested as possible other mainly working-class sites where Hispanic and Anglo-Americans could be found.
    Hamtramck is a minicity community situated within innercity Detroit.   It lies at the center of an area of heavy industry--factories, steel and metal processing plants, and freight yards.   The community covers approximately two square miles and with thirty thousand residents, it is densely populated. While there are some single dwelling houses, the community in general strikes the onlooker as mainly lower working class.
    Hamtramck has long been the nucleus of Greater Detroit's Polish community and until recently was considered essentially a community of Polish and blacks. The dominant group, economically and culturally, is the Polish.   Polish cultural, religious, and social institutions abound, and the major professional, and public service positions (e.g. police and firemen) are still held by those of Polish ancestry.
    More recently Albanians and Arabs have settled in Hamtramck in significant numbers so that the city now has

clear residential areas that are comprised of mainly Polish, black, Albanian, or Arab families. The Albanians have emigrated to the United States via Yugoslavia and Macedonia and many come with the idea that their stay will only be temporary. In describing their group, community leaders stress the facts that Albania has resisted many attempts at colonization, that they are "fiercely proud", that their customs emphasize traditional family roles, with great respect for elders, generous hospitality to guests, and respect for education, even though Albania has long struggled with a very high rate of illiteracy.

The newcomers of Arab extraction came largely from Yemen. Although it is said to have been one of the cradles of early civilization, Yemen has not modernized, and formal education is not developed. As recently as 1976, only 10 percent of Yemen's population was literate. The vast majority are Moslem which means that much attention is given to religion and to Islamic family and social traditions. Family roles are very traditional. For instance, men enjoy more status than women and in general family size enhances the family's status. All these background features characterize the Arab group in Hamtramck.

Thus, Hamtramck's established social structure which was dominantly Polish with a smaller black community, has in the post World War II years experienced basic changes because of the important increases in the number of Albanian and Arabic people who have settled there. The Hamtramck public school system is the only institution that accommodates this ethnic diversity. There are four schools; two elementary, one middle school, and one high school, all of which receive children from all ethnic backgrounds. In 1983 the public school population was approximately 2,350 students, and 678 of these had very limited English language skills.

Pontiac

The second community we studied, Pontiac, is a neighboring but much larger municipality to the north of greater Detroit, similar in its social class makeup to Hamtramck. Pontiac was of particular interest to us because significant numbers of Puerto Rican and Mexican Americans live there. The prominence of these two Hispanic groups throughout the United States made them a valuable addition since we wanted as diversified and as typical a sample of ethnicity as we could manage.

Often Puerto Rican and Mexican Americans are considered simply as "Hispanics", but important historical differences make it mandatory that they be treated as separate ethnic communities. Puerto Rico, for example, maintains a unique relationship as a protectorate of the United States, allowing easy access to the United States mainland and the opportunity to return to Puerto Rico with minimum difficulty and expense. For Mexicans, however, entry to the United States is much more difficult; they have none of the advantages the Puerto Ricans have of being American citizens from birth.

Pontiac is larger than Hamtramck and has, in addition to these two sizable Hispanic communities, large numbers of working-class blacks and whites. The working-class white group includes families transplanted from Kentucky and Tennessee who, for several generations, have come north to work in the automobile factories but who maintain strong links with their native states.

Because of an anomaly in the public school district boundary, a solidly middle-class white community adjacent to Pontiac is served by the Pontiac school board. This allowed us to include, for comparison purposes, a group of middle-class white American parents. Residential area and occupational status were our criteria for placement in the middle-class white group.

One further consideration was the length of residence in the United States of the immigrant minority group members. In our selection procedures, we made sure that all families in our ethnic samples had at least two or more years of living experience in the community or elsewhere in the country. When one compares the length of residence in the United States for all groups involved (with each family drawn at random from separate ethnic lists provided by the schools), there were several interesting outcomes. In Hamtramck, black Americans on the average constitute the oldest resident group (17.89 years) followed by Polish Americans (14.48), Arab-Americans (9.15), and Albanian Americans (7.74). In Pontiac, blacks again constitute the oldest resident group (27 years), followed by the Mexican American (21.73), the white middle-class (19.72), the white working-class (19.33), and finally the Puerto Rican Americans (8.75). Thus, all groups have had at least minimal adjustment time in the United States, and some groups might have a sense of legitimate seniority in the broader community. These are only averages, in later chapters we will examine variances in residence time and relate these to factors such as attitudes towards cultural assimilation and towards multiculturalism, and to maintenance in the home of heritage languages.

METHOD AND PROCEDURES

Respondents.   The participants in this study were parents of children enrolled in public schools in either Hamtramck or Pontiac. The participants were chosen because they belonged to one of the four major ethnic groups who live in Hamtramck (e.g., Polish Americans, Arab Americans, Albanian Americans, and black Americans) or one of the five major groups living in Pontiac (e.g., Mexican Americans, Puerto Rican Americans, black Americans, working-class white Americans, or middle-class white Americans).

Our procedure called for us to select 40 parents from each of the nine different groups in the two communities. The first step was to develop classroom lists indicating all childrens' ethnic backgrounds and then to select at random subsets of children from each of the nine groups. To allow for refusals or cases of incorrect home addresses, we generated lists of 60 names for each target group. Each family received a letter from the appropriate school superintendent which explained the purpose of the study and its potential value.

The socioeconomic backgrounds of the families in all groups are well defined. In Hamtramck most parents work at semiskilled or unskilled jobs, or are unemployed. The vast majority of the children qualify for free noontime lunches at school, and except for a few who live in modest, separate home dwellings, the majority are from subsidized low-rent housing units. The general employment situation in Pontiac was slightly better, but the groups we were dealing with, except for the one middle-class white group, were clearly of working class, semiskilled or unskilled occupational and social class backgrounds.

The sex of the respondent was a particularly thorny issue for our research design. Any hope of finding a scientifically pure, balanced sample of men and women was dashed by the social and cultural realities of the chosen communities. For the Arab and Albanian groups, for instance, it was quite inappropriate to expect to interview mothers, whereas in the black communities, it was mothers and not fathers who were more likely to be available. Thus, our final sample choices are clearly biased in the sense that ethnicity and sex are correlated, making it difficult to draw conclusions about the role of either variable in explaining the overall group differences in attitudes we are to discuss. What we have, therefore, are the views of the acting head of the household.

Research Instrument. Our plan was to search among standard measures of attitudes and values for appropriate and useful scales, and also to develop new measures specifically designed to tap particular combinations of feelings and attitudes. In both cases, the measuring instrument had to be unmistakably straightforward and understandable for use with mainly working class respondents. The instruments also had to be psychometrically sound and so worded that parents would think seriously about certain issues and give us their candid, spontaneous reactions.

The final interview schedule covered a variety of issues, all designed so as to reveal attitudes and feelings about race, language, and culture, and, incidentally, how these might affect the effectiveness and the fairness of public education for their own children. Questions focused on three themes: (1) overall attitudes about cultural and racial diversity in America; (2) attitudes and opinions towards the introduction of heritage languages and heritage cultures into public education; and (3) attitudes and feelings toward specific groups in the community, their own group included.

Once developed and pretested in English, the interview schedule was carefully translated into Arabic, Polish, Albanian, and Spanish and tested again with small samples of representatives of each of the target groups. Because some parents might have had trouble reading, it was decided that the interviewers would ask questions orally and that respondents would give their reactions in terms of numerical scales that accompanied each item. Specifically, every question required a response on a seven-point scale, defined at one end (1) by such qualifiers as "not at all" or "disagree totally", and at the other (7) with "extremely" or "agree totally", with four (4) representing the midpoint on the scale. Thus, the interviews were informal and interpersonal even though the respondents were taken through a predetermined progression of questions so designed that systematic psychometric analyses could be carried out on their responses.

Translation and Interviewing.   To be chosen the interviewers had to be   bilingual in English and the appropriate heritage language.   In addition, each interviewer had to be recognized and respected as a member of one of our target groups.   With the help of language specialists, the research instrument was translated into Polish, Arabic, Albanian, and Spanish.   For the black and white American samples, we pretested with small samples to make sure that the final English version of the schedule was clear and unambiguous.

In choosing the interviewers for the study, we sought out people who themselves were not only members of the appropriate ethnic group and who were bilingual, but who, although more educated, had originally come from the same social class backgrounds as the respondents.   They also had to be sociable and patient people who could communicate and paraphrase easily.   Through discussions with a number of candidates for the work as interviewers, we were able to identify two or more excellent people for each target group.   Many were school teachers, social workers, or prominent people in their respective communities (e.g., the wife of a pastor of an Afro-American church).   These we trained through practice sessions, and, through discussions, we informed them of the purpose of the study. Each of the interviewers then conducted three practice interviews which were analyzed and corrected in follow-up sessions.   Through this interaction, the interviewers got a clear understanding of the significance of each of the questions and how careful they had to be to grasp and accurately record each respondent's responses.

In summary, then, this study is based on the reactions of male and female heads of households who are an integral part of a highly diversified urban center in America.   They are of working class backgrounds; they are identified with a particular ethnic group; with one exception, they are not highly educated or otherwise privileged, and they are all parents of a child at some level, from elementary to high school, in a public school.   The study is not a typical behavioral science survey because it has included hard-to-get adult samples who were interviewed at home.

We see a sharp contrast between this study and those that solicit   attitudes, values, and points of view from college students, school pupils, teachers, or school administrators.   In the present case, we have an opportunity to examine the thinking of parents and families who are personally involved with developing their own modes of coping and competing in a fast-moving multicultural society. The study would not have been possible without the good wishes, interest, and suggestions of school administrators. It also required the collaboration of respected and versatile representatives of the several ethnic subgroups involved because, as interviewers for our study, they could make contact with and relay the meanings of our measuring instruments, and do so in a consistent, reliable manner. The translations into Polish, Arabic, Albanian, and Spanish had to preserve the original meanings, at the same time as they permitted respondents to express themselves in their most comfortable language.

Statistical Procedures. The questionnaire was designed so that 7-point response scales could be used for nearly all questions. Our plan was to apply standard statistical procedures on these response data, using parametric tests of the significance of differences when appropriate and nonparametric tests when, as was the case for many of our analyses, basic assumptions required for parametric tests were not met (see Ferguson, 1981; Siegel, 1956). For instance, on certain questions we found a great deal of within-group consensus wherein the majority of respondents within any one group would respond close to or at the same point on the 7-point scales. This lack of within-group variance made parametric tests inappropriate and forced us to use two types of nonparametric significance tests. For between-group comparisons, we used the Kruskal-Wallis one-way analysis of variance by ranks, a test with a power efficiency of 95.5 percent when compared to the parametric F-test. For within-group comparisons, we used the Wilcoxon matched-pairs signed-ranks test.

Data Presentation. So as not to overwhelm the reader with numbers, the tables of data relevant to each of the following chapters are placed at the end of the chapter. Each data table presents a brief paraphrasing of the complete wording.

3

Ethnic Immigrant Groups in Hamtramck:
Polish, Albanian, and Arab Americans

Our study in Hamtramck included samples of parents
representing the four largest and most visible groups in
the community--those with Polish, Arab, Albanian, and Afro-
American ancestry--and our first data analysis is based on
comparisons among three of these four, those that we will
refer to as "ethnic immigrant" groups.   We examine in
turn each group's point of view regarding the three major
issues of the study: (1) heritage culture maintenance
versus cultural assimilation, (2) maintenance and use of
their heritage language, and (3) their attitudes and social
perceptions of own group and other prominent ethnic groups
in the community.   Then, through comparisons, we highlight
common trends as well as distinctive group idiosyncracies.

THE PERSPECTIVES OF POLISH AMERICAN PARENTS

The basic question all respondents had to take a stand
on was: Should cultural and racial groups give up their
traditional ways of life when they come to America, or
should they maintain their heritage cultures as much as
possible?   The question was carefully and patiently

presented, and once a position was indicated, the respondent was asked a series of follow-up questions to probe the implications of the stance taken. The actual English wording of the main question was:

There is an important debate in America about cultural and racial minority groups. Some people believe that cultural and racial minority groups should give up their traditional ways of life and take on the American way of life, while others believe that cultural and racial minority groups should maintain their traditional ways of life as much as possible when they come to America. Where do you stand in this debate?

Alternative A   **Alternative B**

Cultural and racial   Cultural and racial
minority groups should   minority groups
give up their   **versus**   should maintain
traditional ways of   their ways of life
life and take on the   as much as possible
American way of life.   when they come to
                                           America.

    1   2   3   4   5   6   7
  ____   ____   ____   ____   ____   ____

Agree Strongly   Neutral   Agree Strongly
   with A   with B

An overall picture of the average responses of the three immigrant groups is presented in Figure 3.1. What strikes one first is that none of the three groups actually favors assimilation. Instead all three groups place themselves decidedly toward the multiculturalism end of the continuum, with the means ranging between 5.68 and 6.69, where 4 is the neutral midpoint. This is an important finding and an unexpected one, since the prevailing ideology in many administrative and political institutions in America, including those in the Hamtramck community, is assimilationist. The Polish American group is particularly interesting in its view. Compared to the other ethnic groups in Hamtramck, the Polish Americans, although not quite so polarized in their ratings, still clearly endorse the multiculturalism option.

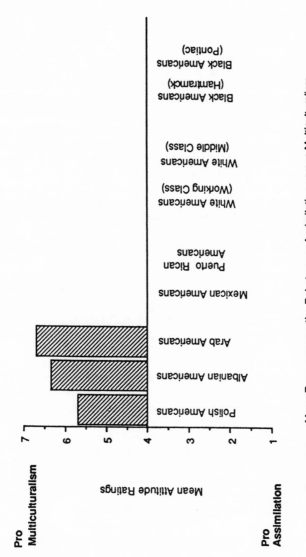

Figure 3.1   Mean Responses on the Debate over Assimilation versus Multiculturalism

The follow-up questions were simplified statements of the basic arguments that are commonly used to either support or refute each major ideology. The mean group responses are given in Table 3.1 which also contains a description of the specific pro/con arguments presented to respondents.

The Polish Americans' reactions to the pro/con arguments are consistent with their favorable stand on the multiculturalism alternative. For instance, they tend to agree that, with assimilation, America loses the best that different groups have to offer, that people will "be robbed" of their identity and that in becoming assimilated (and losing their distinctive ethnicity) they will become hostile towards others. Consistently, they tend to disagree with the arguments that assimilation provides all Americans with a common base for understanding each other through a shared American language and culture, or that America will thereby be unified.

There is, on the other hand, strong agreement with arguments in support of multiculturalism. Our Polish American respondents believe that multiculturalism would help America keep the best that different cultures and races have to offer, that people would thereby be allowed to express their identity, and that they would therefore be open and sympathetic to others. Furthermore, the arguments against multiculturalism are not endorsed: There is no agreement with the viewpoint that multiculturalism would eradicate a common basis for understanding or that America would thereby be divided into disparate, segregated units. There is, nevertheless, a recognition that multiculturalism entails the sustenance of a variety of languages and cultural standards within the nation. It is noteworthy that just as the Polish parents were less extreme than the Arab and Albanian parents in their endorsement of multiculturalism generally, so too were they less extreme than the other two groups in their specific judgments for multiculturalism and against assimilation.

Heritage culture and language: How much is desirable?   If a parental group, like the Polish Americans in this instance, endorses a multicultural ideology, it becomes crucial to explore further what their conception of a multicultural society is. Put in its simplest form, the question becomes: How far should cultural and racial groups in America go in maintaining their cultures and languages? The relevant statistics are presented in Table

3.2.

Cultures and Traditions. When asked specific questions
about heritage culture, Polish American respondents present
one general philosophy and apply it to all cultural groups,
including their own. They reject the notion that cultures
and traditions that are not "American" should be
eliminated. When asked whether ethnic groups should keep
their own styles of food, dress, songs, and dance, Polish
respondents agree that they should. Similarly, the idea
that a group should maintain its cultural values (including
child rearing values), and attend courses about its history
and traditions in church-run or community-run classes is
accepted at least to a moderate degree.
     The fifth item in the series asks whether cultural and
racial groups should have courses about their own cultural
history and traditions provided by public schools. Here
the Polish respondents are also in moderate agreement and
even the final item asking about giving <u>equal</u> <u>time</u> in
schools to each group's cultural history and traditions as
is given to American history and traditions also prompts a
moderate and reserved endorsement.
     Since the Polish American parents were asked these
questions about other ethnic groups in the community as
well as their own, the results show clearly that they
present a generalized favorable view about culture and
language maintenance (i.e., a view that is applied to other
ethnic groups as well as their own).

Heritage Languages. A parallel set of questions was then
asked specifically about how extensively heritage languages
should be used. The parental responses are presented in
Table 3.3. As on the culture issue, Polish American parents
are, not surprisingly, more favorable to relatively modest
proposals for language use and maintenance and they become
gradually less favorable to more extreme proposals, such as
providing equal time for the use of ethnic languages as is
provided for English as an instructional medium in the
school system. Thus, when asked if cultural groups whose
language is not standard English should stop using that
language, Polish respondents disagree. When asked if
ethnic groups should use their own language for festival
days, cultural songs, traditional stories, prayers and
religious services, the Polish sample is in moderate
agreement. Similarly, the Polish sample is in moderate
agreement for speaking with older family members, speaking

within the family, learning to read and write their heritage languages through church-run or community-run classes, and finally for using heritage languages as part of the teaching and learning process in public schools.

In all cases, the Polish respondents display moderate agreement. The last, and what we thought would be an extreme proposition, that of equal instructional time in a heritage language, provokes more reserve, but more a neutral reaction than an outright rejection. Our hierarchy of questions may have hit a tolerance point for the Polish American parents, but we knew of no more extreme question to ask to test the real limits of this issue. In any case, the consistency and orderliness of the patterns of responses are clear. As items progress from moderate proposals to more radical ones, the tendency to endorse decreases regularly.

There is then a fairly clear answer in the reactions of these parents on how far groups should go in maintaining their cultural traditions and their heritage languages. For Polish parents the preferred options, for themselves and other groups, is to maintain heritage cultures and languages through the home environment, and this is reasonable since heritage culture and language are associated with home and family more than with the broader public areas of American life. At the same time, it is clear that the Polish respondents are favorably disposed toward all levels of maintenance, including some public school involvement in teaching heritage languages and teaching about heritage cultures.

Of special interest is the fact that the Polish parents do not reject outright the idea of having significant portions of the school day allotted to teaching via a heritage language. What might prompt immigrant parents to feel that American public schools should be involved in maintaining or developing skills in any number of heritage languages? Why not take care of such needs either at home or in church or in ethnic community centers? From discussions we have had with educators in the Hamtramck system, three explanations surface. One is that endorsement of a heritage language by the public school would have a positive effect on many levels. It would support parental desires, it would bolster group self-views in the community, and it would support attempts to develop a bicultural identity in children. Offering heritage language instruction in public schools would bring the linguistic feature of a group's ethnicity out of the closet and it would enhance ethnic pride.   Second, providing part of the instruction through heritage languages would ensure that those children who are not advanced enough in English would be able to keep up and compete with Anglophone pupils in the content details of educational matters such as math, science, or social studies.   Thus, although it is recognized that all this is very probably asking too much from an American public school system, it is also recognized that the use of heritage languages could have various beneficial effects.

Of course our Polish American parents may simply be expressing a generally positive attitude about language maintenance, not necessarily supporting how that should be accomplished.   That is, they may not have thought through all the pedagogical consequences of having heritage languages used half the time in school.   Instead they may have endorsed the item simply as a means of expressing their strong desire for the heritage language to remain alive.   Nevertheless, they would like it in the school.

Maintenance and Use of the Heritage Language: Polish American Views

The Choice: Heritage Language, English, Bilingualism. Language is the most visible and salient component of multiculturalism, the component that has a direct impact on performance in school subjects, and on the makeup of educational policies.   For language minority groups, the school plays a major role.   It can help ethnic children learn English; it can encourage or discourage the use of the heritage language , and thus it can control the fate of children's potential to be fluently bilingual.   For native English-speaking children, the school determines whether or not they learn some other language, whether it be a world language or the language of a cultural group living in the same community.

In order to examine views about this pivotal feature of multiculturalism, parents were asked to evaluate and then examine the consequences of three alternatives: their son or daughter becoming fluent in English only, becoming fluent in the heritage language only, or becoming fluently bilingual. Specifically, Polish parents were asked to imagine what the consequences would be if their child mastered only English, mastered only Polish, or became bilingual in English and Polish.

The group reactions to these alternatives are given in Table 3.4 which also lists the specific questions asked. It is clear that "positive consequences" would be anticipated if children either became bilingual, or mastered English only. There is nothing positive to having children dominant in Polish only. In fact, a son or daughter who is fluent in Polish only is seen in an unfavorable light generally and is considered less likely to be successful. The Polish parents therefore believe that if their children became either bilingual or mastered English only, the children would feel more accepted in America. They would be more open and relaxed with others, not stand out as different, nor be treated as second-class citizens as they might be if they only spoke Polish.

When asked if language skills would affect their children's sympathy towards other cultural and racial groups in America, Polish parents as a group believe their children would be relatively sympathetic towards others regardless of their skills in English and/or Polish. If they were bilingual, or unilingual in English, however, their children would feel more pride in themselves, would bring more status and respect to their group, and would be happier than if they mastered Polish only.

The same parental views hold up for concrete, bread-and-butter issues. Children who master English only or become bilingual are seen as being more intelligent, as more likely to get good marks in school, and as having better chances for certain jobs. In other words, there are both instrumental and social advantages to mastering English or developing a strong bilinguality through Polish and English.

The more interesting question then arises: Are there substantial advantages for a Polish American child who is fluent in both Polish and English over one who is fluent in English only? The answer is "yes", and the advantages again appear to be practical and economic as well as social (see Table 3.4). Thus, Polish-English bilingual children are more likely to make their parents happy, more likely to bring status and respect to the Polish group, and more likely to show intelligence compared to those who would master English only. Success on the job market is the most striking and perhaps most informative difference between the two groups: for those who speak Polish and English the mean score is 5.71, while for those who speak only English the mean score is 4.55. Polish parents as a group, therefore, believe bilingualism is more than simply a tool for the idealistic "appreciation" of another culture. They see it also as clearly relevant to the hard realities of the world of work.

Attitudes Towards Own and Other Ethnic Groups: Polish American Parents

Both sides of the maintain versus assimilate debate have as their rationale an improvement in harmonious relations between and among the various ethnic groups that make up a complex pluralistic society such as the United States.   The perspective of the proassimilation side is that if emphasis is placed on those features all people have in common--that we are all Americans--rather than on our cultural and linguistic differences, the more harmonious the social climate would be.   Similarly, the arguments for cultural/linguistic maintenance hinge on intergroup harmony derived from the freedom that could be extended to all ethnic groups to maintain what is unique about their cultural backgrounds while taking on the essential features of the host nation's culture.   One position is energized by worries about antagonisms and split allegiances while the other is fueled by worries about losing or being stripped of an essential personal allegiance and an identity.   Furthermore, one position implies that juggling two cultural orientations is too difficult a social demand while the other views the juggling act as both manageable and necessary because it is the only way to avoid losing a cultural identity.

How much intergroup harmony do we find in Hamtramck, a setting where the American pressures to assimilate are as strong as anywhere else but where the three groups we have in focus have all opted for the maintenance alternative? We tried to get an answer to this central question by probing each group's attitudes towards all major ethnic groups in the community and by soliciting their conception of social distance and where each community group fits in that conception.

Attitudes. As a measure of intergroup attitudes, we presented each parent with a list of general personality characteristics that one might easily ascribe to any ethnic group. The list itself and the average ratings made by our respondents are in Table 3.5.   Note that in this case we include the black Americans as a fourth group in the include the black Americans as a fourth group in the comparisons because they become a critical part of the intergroup network of attitudes.

The mean ratings given by our Polish American parents indicate that they have a solidly positive image of their own group. They see Polish Americans as more trustworthy, more intelligent, and more law abiding than any other group in the comparison. We interpret this pattern as a reflection of a strong and positive own-group pride. More important, however, the ratings these Polish parents assign to other groups, while not as pronounced, are nonetheless favorable. It is only the black American group that is singled out as being less hardworking than the other groups and, along with the Albanians, as being somewhat more violent and aggressive. On the other hand, blacks are viewed as more likable, generally, than the Arabs or Albanians. Overall, the Polish American respondents single out no particular group as a target for generalized prejudice. Rather, all groups are viewed as only somewhat less desirable than members of their own ethnic group.

The scales asking for judgments of how similar each other group is to one's own, present a particularly interesting, but disquieting profile. The importance of this scale lies in the often validated finding that people are attracted to those judged as similar to themselves, suggesting that those seen as different are not likely candidates for close relationships. What emerges here is that our Polish American respondents have a positive own-group image and are generally sympathetic to other ethnic groups at the same time as they distance themselves somewhat from these other ethnic groups in terms of similarity ratings. As we will see, this same tendency shows up in the social distance ratings to be described below.

Since these intergroup attitudes come in networks, we can ask: How is the Polish community viewed by the other groups in Hamtramck? In the first place, other ethnic groups do not share the very positive attitudes Polish people have of themselves. In terms of being likable, for example, the 6 and 7 ratings Polish respondents gave themselves become 3 and 4 for Arab and Albanian respondents. Thus, just as the Polish rated other groups with some reserve (3, 4, and 5 ratings), this reserve is reciprocated by these same groups. The black respondents' ratings of the Polish community are of special interest, as we will elaborate in a later chapter. Briefly, they

they consider to be especially hardworking, intelligent, smart, and law abiding. At the same time, there is some envy or resentment registered since, compared to their own group,   black Americans see Polish Americans as much less unfairly treated despite being no more intelligent, smart, or law abiding than themselves. Also, Polish Americans are viewed as being very different from blacks and somewhat less American. Since the Polish community is the best established one in Hamtramck, the more recently arrived Arab and Albanian respondents may well expect those of Polish background to be well represented in the economic and political structure of Hamtramck. Blacks, on the other hand, have a long history of being American, and hence their reaction to Polish Americans is ambivalent, basically favorable but tinged with envy and resentment, features not expressed by the ethnic immigrant groups.

Social distance. The attitudes of the Polish respondents towards their own and other ethnic groups are captured in another fashion through the social distance scale which asks respondents to indicate how willing they would be to accept members of a particular group in a variety of social contexts, e.g., as partners in marriage, as neighbors, or as co-workers. The group responses are presented in Table 3.6.

Polish American respondents say they would be very willing to interact with other Poles at all stages of social distance, as would be expected. They are much less willing to accept members of the other groups, however, and the pattern of their reactions is consistent--the more intimate the relationship, the less accepting they are. Nonetheless, there is an interesting and important reversal in the expected order of the steps of the social distance scale. It turns out that having a member of a particular group as a neighbor ranks closer to the intimate end than does having that person as a close friend. In other words, there is more exclusivity associated with neighbor than with close friend. Reversals of this sort have been found before in cross-cultural studies (see Lambert, 1952; Silverman & Cochrane, 1972; Moe, Nacoste & Insko, 1981), and they usually make good sociological sense.   The apparent paradox here also makes sense in the context of the important and highly publicized role that ethnically mixed neighborhoods played in the period of heightened racial tensions during the Civil Rights movement of the 1960s and early 1970s in the United States. Detroit was one of the major urban centers involved in racial uprisings in that period.   Thus, when questioned about the possibility of other ethnic groups becoming neighbors, our Polish respondents may have been expressing fears about security and about the effects mixed neighborhoods might have on property values.

Aside from this one reversal, the expected relationship between the degree of social intimacy and the willingness for interaction holds. Within this pattern, it is instructive to examine the point at which the ratings take a more dramatic shift in the direction of exclusion. The most exclusive step in social distance is accepting a member of another group into one's family through marriage. For the Polish parents, these are the only ratings that fall on the not willing side of the seven point scale. Apparently, for Polish American parents, marriage outside the group would be going against a powerful norm.   The social basis for this norm could well be a perception on the part of members of the Polish ethnic group that its very existence as a distinct cultural or racial group, which has only finite numbers, depends upon within-group marriages. Or it may simply be that these parents do not see any economic advantage for their children if they were to marry a member of a relatively less powerful and less financially secure group.

Although Polish respondents give essentially similar ratings on the social distance scale for Albanians, Arabs, and blacks, there are subtle differences in their reactions to blacks.   Blacks receive relatively unfavorable ratings on the marriage (M = 2.16) and neighbor items (M = 3.58), but relatively favorable ratings on the friendship (M = 4.10), co-worker (M = 4.84), and citizen (M = 5.39) items. Poles appear to view blacks in a very specific manner: relations with them can be very good so long as blacks remain within specified roles. Were blacks to overstep the acceptable roles, the reactions of Polish respondents would likely become relatively negative. This is probably what is meant by the statement that minority groups "should keep their place".

THE PERSPECTIVES OF ALBANIAN AMERICAN PARENTS

The Albanians comprise one of the vibrant, recently arrived ethnic groups trying to make a place for themselves among the more established Polish residents of Hamtramck and more generally in the United States. All told, there are less than eigthy thousand Albanians in the entire United States, and Albania and Yugoslavia, the countries of origin of this group, are little known to most Americans. Because of the strangeness of these people and their ways, it is not surprising that other ethnic groups are puzzled about Albanians, particularly about their goals and their means of attaining goals. Here we examine and compare the perspectives and attitudes of Albanian parents through their responses to our three major questions.

Heritage Culture Maintenance versus Assimilation: Albanian American Parents

We have already noted in Figure 3.1 where the Albanian parents stand on the debate about assimilation versus multiculturalism in relation to the other prominent ethnic groups in Hamtramck. Albanian parents are very much in favor of all ethnic groups in America maintaining their cultural traditions. Their strong endorsement of multiculturalism is also registered in their assessments of the arguments for and against multiculturalism (see Table 3.1). In their eyes, multiculturalism would permit ethnic groups to retain the best that each has to offer the United States, to be open and sympathetic towards other ethnic groups, and to express important aspects of personal identities. There is no endorsement of the argument that multiculturalism would divide America, or that it would eliminate a common basis for understanding among Americans. The Albanian American respondents nevertheless recognize that a multicultural policy would make America multilingual. On the other hand, if ethnic groups were to give up their cultural traditions, Albanian parents would anticipate several negative consequences: group members would likely be hostile to other groups, America would lose the best that different groups have to offer, and individuals would lose an important aspect of their identity. At the same time, Albanian parents recognize some of the potential advantages of a policy of assimilation: from a broad perspective, assimilation might help America be unified, it would provide a common set of values and a common language for communication.

Heritage Culture and Language: How Much is Desirable?
Our sample of Albanian parents seems strongly committed to
a multicultural ideology.   How far do they believe their
group should go in the maintenance of culture and language
in America?   The reactions are tabulated in Tables 3.2 and
3.3.   First, they are slightly more committed to
maintaining culture and language than are our Polish
parents.   They reject the idea that culture and language
should not be maintained, and there is a very strong
endorsement of maintenance at each step of our scale
(except one), placing them at least one step beyond the
Polish parents.   For instance, Albanian parents feel more
strongly that courses on culture and language should be
taught in   church and community-run classes. In other
words, while Polish parents showed some inclination to
restrict their own culture and language to the home,
Albanian parents feel that their traditions and language
deserve attention beyond the home, at least into their own
ethnic community.   The one exception is the proposition
that half of public school time be spent on Albanian
culture and language in which case they are neutral, as was
the case with the Polish respondents.
    Supplemental analyses also indicate that Albanian
American parents, like those in the other ethnic groups,
feel that what is fair or right for their own group is also
appropriate for other ethnolinguistic groups.   There is, in
other words, no evidence of cultural chauvinism of the sort
that leads to beliefs that one's own culture and language
should be maintained but not the cultures and languages of
other ethnic groups.

**Maintenance and Use of the Heritage Language:
Albanian American Parents**

The Choice: Heritage Language, English, Bilingualism.
What would the consequences be for Albanian American
children if they were to be monolingual versus bilingual?
When asked to imagine that their child might become either
fluent in English only, fluent in Albanian only, or fluent
in both English and Albanian, parental reactions are clear
and consistent (see Table 3.4).   Being able to speak
Albanian only in America is perceived as a handicap, a
reaction much like that given by the Polish American
parents.   That alternative would be a handicap for getting
a good job or good grades at school.   On a social level,

children with Albanian only would not be considered as intelligent, and the status of their group in the broader community would suffer. Furthermore, children limited to the Albanian language only would not make their parents happy, would not feel relaxed with others, would not have self pride, nor be truly accepted in America.

On the other hand, having a mastery of English only, while more advantageous than mastering Albanian only, is nevertheless not perceived as ideal. Granting that unilingual English skills would be essential in America, Albanian parents see only modest practical and social gains for that alternative. For them, the most desirable alternative by far is to have their children fluent in both Albanian and English. The practical advantages of that type of bilinguality are judged to be considerable: it would reflect a high degree of intelligence, would promote better grades in school, and open access to more and better jobs. Rather than being treated as different or as a second-class citizens, if bilingual, their children would feel comfortable in the community, would have more pride in themselves, bring status to their group and would make their parents happy.

In summary, the consequences of being bilingual are judged to be even more desirable for the Albanian parents than was the case for the Polish parents. Again the striking feature of the Albanian perspective is that bilingualism not only maintains important links with ethnolinguistic heritages but also, at a very pragmatic level, it facilitates school performance and employment opportunities.

Attitudes Towards Own and Other Ethnic Groups: Albanian American Parents

Attitudes. The attitudes of Albanian parents toward their own and other ethnic groups in the community are presented in Table 3.5. As noted earlier, the Albanians are newly arrived and relatively less experienced in coping with America and with other Americans. Nonetheless, they apparently maintain a very positive self-image. They judge their own group to be by far the most likable, trustworthy, and hardworking. This positive self-image, however, may disguise some defensiveness, judging from their reaction to other groups, for in general they are not as generous as the Polish parents in their ratings of other groups. Black

Americans in particular are rated quite unfavorably on a number of dimensions, not only on the major evaluative dimensions, but also on personal dimensions referring to intelligence, aggression, being American, and law-abiding.

The similar to me scale is of particular significance because of its link to the attractiveness of others in the community. Albanian respondents see Polish Americans as somewhat similar to themselves, Arab Americans as moderately so only, and black Americans as very different. From the Albanian American perspective, there are few signs that open and friendly relations with blacks are likely and only faint hopes for positive relations with Poles and Arabs.

Social distance. The general attitudes of Albanian parents towards other groups in the community are reflected just as clearly in their social distance ratings (see Table 3.6). Albanian parents seem extremely exclusive with respect to social interactions with other groups. They unmistakably eliminate Poles, Arabs, and blacks as candidates for entry into the family through marriage, and although they are more open to contacts of a friendship, neighbor and co-worker sort with these three groups, they nonetheless keep blacks and Arab Americans at a sizable social distance even on these dimensions.

THE PERSPECTIVES OF ARAB AMERICAN PARENTS

The Arab respondents, like the Albanians, are also relatively recent arrivals who are making their own contributions to the ethnic, racial and linguistic makeup of Hamtramck. The Yemen Arab group in Hamtramck, though highly visible, is nevertheless quite small, and this forced us to extend our selection of parents beyond the borders of Hamtramck in order to complete our desired sample size of forty. The other parents included were also from Yemen and lived in Ann Arbor, a separate community about an hour's drive from Hamtramck. These parents were selected so as to be from similar social class, occupational, and educational backgrounds as those from Hamtramck.

Here we examine the total group's perspectives and attitudes, and relate them to the two other major ethnic groups in Hamtramck.

Heritage Culture Maintenance versus Assimilation: Arab American Parents

Arab parents' views on the fundamental debate question are presented in Figure 3.1, which shows that although all three ethnic groups favour multiculturalism, the Arab sample is the most committed to that ideology. Since they give the strongest endorsement of multiculturalism, we would expect them to reflect the same views in their assessments of specific arguments for and against the maintenance of cultural and racial diversity, and this is indeed the case. As shown in Table 3.1, Arab parents, even more than the others, believe that giving up one's heritage culture and language would mean that the nation as a whole would lose the best that different ethnic groups have to offer, that the ethnic groups themselves would be deprived of an important part of their identity, and that this deprivation would lead them to be hostile toward others. Like the other parental groups, the Arab parents are not convinced that giving up their traditions would help make America unified or that having one national language would provide a common base for mutual understanding.

In contrast the Arab American parents see a number of favorable consequences for maintaining heritage cultures and languages, although certain reservations are expressed. On the positive side, their position is that, by encouraging multiculturalism, America would keep the best that different groups have to offer, and that people would be better able to express their identity. Nonetheless, this might not mean that each group would be totally sympathetic to other ethnic groups. In their view, generalized sympathy is not a certain guaranteed consequence of keeping heritage languages and cultures alive and active.

At the same time, Arab American parents see no negative consequences associated with maintaining languages other than English. Their position is that multilanguage maintenance would not detract from mutual undertstanding nor from national unity in America, even though it would make America multilingual.

Heritage Culture and Language: How Much is Desirable? Not only do Arabic American parents endorse a multicultural ideology, they also show consistent support for the arguments that favor multiculturalism over cultural and

linguistic assimilation.   How far do Arab parents think
ethnic groups should go in the maintenance of their
cultures and languages?   The data are given in Tables 3.2
and 3.3.   In one respect they resemble our other parental
groups in that they also reserve their highest ratings for
use of the heritage language within the family.   Beyond
this similarity, however, Arab parents endorse more
strongly than others the use of their heritage language in
the community and in public schools.   Moreover, Arab
parents feel that all ethnic groups should be able to use
the native language beyond the family confines.   Thus, we
have further evidence from our Arab American respondents
that broad abstract ideologies about cultural diversity
translate directly into the desire for concrete steps to be
taken to maintain ethnic cultures and languages, one's own
as well as those of other ethnolinguistic groups.

**Maintenance and Use of the Heritage Language: Arab
American Parents**

The Choice: Heritage Language, English, Bilingualism.
Since most of the parents in our Arab sample, while fluent
in Arabic, have also developed considerable skill in
English, their thoughts about having their children become
bilingual are of special interest. Which alternative would
be most attractive: having their children fluent in Arabic
only, fluent in standard English only, or fluently
bilingual in Arabic and English?   The responses of Arab
parents to these questions resemble closely those of the
Albanians (see Table 3.4). First, they recognize that a
mastery of Arabic only would be a great disadvantage for
their children in America. It would make them stand out as
different, and they would suffer a social stigma within the
family, within their own community, and in the larger
American context. As well, they would lose out in the
competitive job market.
     Speaking English has great advantages but not if
fluency in Arabic suffers. The idea that their children
would master English only, although significantly more
attractive than knowing Arabic only, is not as pleasing an
alternative as becoming bilingual in English and Arabic.
The favorable consequences of becoming bilingual extend
beyond a sense of family and group pride and overall social
adjustment to advantages in the bread-and-butter economic
domain as well.

Arab American Attitudes Towards Own and Other Ethnic Groups

Attitudes.   Members of the Arab American community in Hamtramck are   relatively recent arrivals and like our Albanian respondents, they worry about identity loss and a confusion in self-image.   In the Albanian case, however, the issue is complicated because most Americans know little about Albania or Albanian people.   For Arab Americans the issue is one of extensive and controversial mass media exposure.   This excess of information about the Arab world has undoubtedly contributed to the phenomenon of "Arab-bashing" referred to earlier.

As is evident in Table 3.5, our sample of Arab American parents project a profile of attitudes similar to that of the Albanian sample, with even more ethnocentrism evident.   As a group, they present a relatively positive self-image, although one not quite as favorable as that of Polish parents.   However, in their attitudes towards other groups, Arab parents are less than generous in their ratings of Polish people and Albanians, and they are distinctly negative in their views of blacks.

Social Distance.   The same relatively suspicious attitude toward other ethnic groups coupled with ethnocentrism is evident as well in their social distance ratings (see Table 3.6).   Not only is family membership exclusively limited to other Arabs, but for friendships,   neighbors, and co-workers as well, the Arab parents keep all other ethnic groups at a distance, even the Polish Americans who as a group are decidedly more generous towards Arabs than the reverse.   In fact, Arab American parents make little differentiation among Polish, Albanians, or blacks in terms of social distance.   It could be that this more pronounced ethnocentric attitude is sensed by the other ethnic groups in the community, since each of them, the Polish included, place Arab Americans at relatively distant positions on the scales, similar to their placements of blacks.   There is a difficult problem of interpretation here, however, because it could be that Arab Americans sense that others keep them at a distance and thus retrench with an ethnocentric posture.   Or it could be the other way around, and only further detailed research could clarify this important issue.

Parental Value Orientations and Expectations for their Children: Cross-Group Comparisons

If we take stock at this point, what we have found in Hamtramck is a consistent pattern of reciprocal ethnic group cleavage and ethnocentrism involving the three major ethnic immigrant groups, each group holding very favorable own-group views that are not reciprocated with the same generosity or intensity by the other ethnic groups in the community.   In certain cases, for instance the Polish American parents, the extent of own-group pride and apparent comfort with ethnic identity seem within normal boundaries.   And the Polish American views of other groups, although less favorable than self-views, are far from being hostile.   In the cases of the Albanian and Arabic respondents, however, the cleavage and social distancing from other groups is sharp and strong.

Since all three ethnic groups had expressed a clear desire to maintain their distinctive ethnic and linguistic identities, one begins to wonder about the everyday state of intergroup harmony in Hamtramck and in what direction intergroup relations are headed in that community.   Some would argue that what we have seen is typical and to be expected.   The general social pressures in America for cultural assimilation normally promote these types and degrees of social tension, especially for newly arrived ethnolinguistic groups, but, over time, these pressures will promote   assimilation and its associated sense of unity.   Others with a multiculturalism alternative in mind would argue that such tensions can only be reduced by a social policy that permits each ethnic group to be assured of the persistence of its unique identity and comfortable as   one   group   contributing   to   a   strong multicultural/multilingual identity for the nation as a whole.

But these basic ideological differences take time to manifest   themselves in one direction or the other.   We wanted to know what other concurrent processes might be at play in this presumably typical urban American setting that might promote the interethnic group ethnocentrism that is apparent in the reactions of at least two of the three parental groups studied.   For example, do these three ethnic groups clash in terms of basic value systems?   Might they have discordant perspectives on how children should be brought up or how they should be educated?   Since all respondents were parents with children in public schools, the concerns about training and educating children should be common ones, even if the preferred modes of educating young people differ. Furthermore, do these three groups of parents have different conceptions of the work world and their children's place in it that separate them from one another?

With questions like these in mind, we were prompted to go somewhat deeper into parents' value orientations, and into the expectations each parental group has for its children. In other words, we wanted to explore in a very preliminary way whether these groups were on essentially centrifugal value trajectories, wanting and expecting basically incompatible things from life in America for their families, especially their children, or if they were fundamentally in agreement on these important background issues.

Value Orientations

We anticipated that the differences in values might contribute indirectly to intergroup tension and thus we included measures of values in our plans for interviewing. One respected and often used mode of assessing the basic values of cultural groups is a scale developed by Florence Kluckhohn (1950). It highlights three supposedly fundamental outlooks on life that are believed to be especially relevant for survival in an achievement oriented society like America. The following descriptions of these three orientations are taken from Rosen (1959) who also used the Kluckhohn scales in an important cross-cultural study.

1. An **Activistic-Passivistic Orientation** concerns the extent to which the culture of a group encourages the individual to believe in the possibility of his manipulating the physical and social environment to his advantage. An activistic culture encourages the individual to believe that it is both possible and necessary for him to improve his status, whereas a passivistic culture promotes the acceptance of the notion that individual efforts to achieve mobility are relatively futile.

2. An **Individualistic-Collectivistic Orientation** refers to the extent to which the individual is expected to subordinate his needs to the group. This

orientation is specifically concerned with the degree
to which the society expects the individual to
maintain close physical proximity to his family of
orientation, even at the risk of limiting vocational
opportunities; and the degree to which the society
emphasizes group incentives rather than personal
rewards. The collectivistic society places a greater
stress than the individualistic on group ties and
group incentives.

3. A   Present-Future Orientation concerns the
society's attitude toward time and its impact upon
behavior.   A present oriented society stresses the
merit of living in the present, emphasizing immediate
gratifications; a future oriented society encourages
the belief that planning and present sacrifices are
worthwhile, or morally obligatory, in order to insure
future gains. (Rosen, 1959, 54-55).

    The items of the Kluckhohn scale are presented in
Table 3.7 along with the responses of the parents. Here we
find certain rather striking contrasts on particular
issues.   For instance, the Arab American respondents,
relative to the Polish and Albanians, are most favorable to
the idea of residing close to parents and of being part of
an organization rather than seeking individual recognition.
This makes them markedly on the collectivistic, non
individualistic extreme of this bipolar dimension.   The
Arabs are also most fatalistic, placing themselves more
toward the passivistic end of the passivism-activism
dimension than either the Albanian or Polish respondents.
The Albanians are distinctive in terms of their emphasis on
security in occupational choice, being content with what
comes one's way in life, and the futility of planning
ahead.
    These comparisons suggest that there may well be quite
different   philosophies of life and expectancies involved
in the thinking of these three ethnic groups.   But, of
course, much more detailed research specifically on such
values would be needed to fully understand the role such
philosophies might be playing here.   The more important
question, however, is whether these differences, pronounced
as certain of them are, need necessarily promote disharmony
or whether they might pass as simply interesting contrasts,
no more alarmingly divergent than differences that exist

among established American groups who differ in religious convictions or who represent the interests of different age or social class groups.

Attitudes Towards Public Education

Since all of our respondents were parents with a son or daughter in the public school system, and since children from all ethnic groups come together in public schools, we collected detailed opinions about several facets of education that might elucidate agreement or discord among our three parental groups in terms of educational expectations.

The first series of questions dealt with the importance of education. The results are summarized in Table 3.8. The Polish, Albanian, and Arabic respondents are in full agreement that education is extremely important, and that, if anything, more education is needed. High school education, they all agree, is just not an adequate preparation for decent employment.

The Structure of Public Schools. In terms of the structure of public schools (Table 3.8), the Polish American respondents, the Arab Americans, and the Albanian Americans favor cultural and racial diversity in the classroom. All three groups also agree on the importance of discipline in schooling.

As to the mixing of sexes in school, the Polish respondents favor having boys and girls in the same classroom--the usual and apparently accepted American procedure--and they are favorably disposed to promoting interaction between the sexes in the school context. Interestingly, this conventional attitude is not at all favored by the Arab and Albanian respondents who strongly endorse segregation of the sexes. This then represents a sharp contrast and another possible source of value clash.

The Roles of Teachers, Students, and Parents in Public Education. On this set of questions (Table 3.8), the Polish American respondents generally agree that teachers nowadays are not as devoted to students as they used to be, making them similar to the Arab respondents, but different from the Albanians who are much harsher in their implicit criticism of teachers. The same pattern emerges on the question of students' devotion to learning--the Polish and

the   Arab Americans are of the opinion that children are
not as interested in learning as they used to be, but their
opinion in both cases is much less extreme than that of the
Albanian respondents.

In other respects, the Polish American parents are less
critical of the school system and of parental involvement
in education than are the Albanian parents. Overall, the
Albanian parental group stands apart in its beliefs that
the school should exert much more discipline, that neither
teachers nor students are as dedicated to the task of
education as they used to be, that parents do not show
enough interest in their children's education, and that
schools do not give parents the opportunity to participate.
The Albanian profile, therefore, is a very demanding one
that strikes us as authoritarian in nature. And, there is
no doubt that Albanian children are fully aware of their
parents' perspectives on these issues.

In contrast to both the Albanian and Polish American
parents, the Arab American respondents are not as
dissatisfied with the efforts and the offerings of various
school personnel. They feel that they, as parents, are
interested in their children's education and that the
school provides parents with opportunities to express their
views. Like the other two groups, the Arab Americans
believe more discipline is called for in school, but they
feel teachers are devoted to their task and that students
are at least minimally motivated.

The Relative Importance of Various Curriculum Subjects. A
series of questions probed for parents' opinions about the
relative importance of various school subjects. The
results are summarized in Table 3.9. For all three
samples, the most important academic subjects are
mathematics, science, computer science, and practical
training. All groups also rate English language arts and
American history highly. Ethnic group differences emerge
on the questions dealing with language and culture. The
Arab and the Albanian American parents believe that the
study of their own languages and histories is very
important, while the Polish American parents feel that the
study of the Polish language and Polish history are
relatively less important. A similar pattern emerges for
the importance of learning other foreign languages, such as
French or Spanish, and the history of foreign nations. In
both cases, the Polish parents say that such study has less
importance than do the Arab or the Albanian parents.

On the matter of sex education the Polish respondents acknowledge its importance and this places them in sharp contrast to Arab and Albanian respondents who reject sex education out of hand.

Parents' Views of the World of Work.   When asked more specific questions about job aspirations for their sons and/or daughters and the likelihood of these aspirations being attained, Polish parents, not surprisingly, would be extremely happy if their sons or daughters succeeded in a major professional occupation, and the pattern of responses descends predictably in keeping with the status of the occupations considered (see Table 3.10). Of interest are the points at which there is a significant shift in ratings of satisfaction.   There is appreciable decline from "major professional" occupations to "minor   professional" occupations to "skilled" to "semiskilled" worker, and from "semiskilled" to "unskilled" worker.   Thus, the Polish parents say they would be happy if their sons or daughters could obtain employment as a skilled worker or better.

When asked about the likelihood that their children will actually secure a job in one of the five status categories, Polish American parents appear both realistic and resigned.   That is, "skilled worker" is seen as the most probable occupational category for their children, with the lower and higher status positions decreasing in probability of attainment.   However, none of the job categories is seen as highly unlikely, indicating that reality is coupled with a certain optimism.

The occupational aspirations Albanian parents have for their children are distinctive in certain regards.   Like the two other ethnic groups, Albanian parents would be progressively happier the higher the status of the occupational level achieved by their children.   However, they would be far less happy than the other parental groups if their children were to not end up in either a major, or at least, a minor professional occupation.   Indeed, the idea that their children might become semiskilled, or unskilled workers evokes a negative reaction, something not reflected by the two other parental groups.   These satisfaction ratings are associated directly with the likelihood they see of their children ending up at various occupational levels: Albanian parents feel that there is little chance of their children becoming unskilled, semiskilled or even skilled workers.   Instead they believe it is highly probable that their children will attain high level positions.   Thus, the Albanian parents project a strong concern for high achievement on the part of their children and they hold very high aspirations (and probably unrealistic ones) for their children in the world of work.

The Arab American parents also seem relatively demanding of their children.   They would be most happy, of course, if their son or daughter were successful in securing a major or minor professional job.   However, they do not like the prospect of their children becoming semiskilled or unskilled workers.   In this sense they resemble the Albanian parents and contrast with the Polish parents who are more ready to accept a wider range of occupational status for their children.

When asked about the likelihood of their children obtaining various levels of jobs, the Arab parents present a unique profile: they are the only ethnic group of the three in Hamtramck that expects their children to end up with an unskilled or semiskilled job.   This places them in a dilemma however, because they are not optimistic about their children's occupational future and yet they anticipate disappointment should their children end up with relatively low status jobs.

IN PERSPECTIVE

Our samples of Polish American, Arab American, and Albanian American parents are all strongly committed to the idea of multiculturalism and they all reject assimilation as a viable alternative for newcomers to America.   The Polish parents, while not as extreme as the two other groups, nevertheless show a surprisingly strong endorsement of multiculturalism when one considers that many of this group are third generation Polish American residents.

As well, parents from all three groups are firm in their belief that being bilingual in the heritage language and English would be a great advantage for their children. The advantages they see are not limited to feelings of ethnic identity and family solidarity but extend to anticipated advantages in the world of work.   Furthermore, all are in agreement that the important subjects at school are mathematics, science, computer technology, and practical skills, suggesting that they realize fully what preparations are necessary for their children if they want to succeed in the American system.

Along with these fundamental similarities, certain key

ethnic group differences in perspective emerge. The Polish parents are not quite as committed to multiculturalism and not as extreme on the maintenance of heritage languages. Instead, they present a constellation of attitudes that would be expected of a group with a long-standing and relatively secure status within the Hamtramck community. They have a positive self-image, they are optimistic but realistic in their aspirations for their children, and they tend to be relatively tolerant in showing less of a tendency to stereotype and categorize ethnic groups. They, in other words, appear to have adjusted to American norms, and they have learned how to survive.

The Albanian and Arab parents give indications, mainly through the more extreme stands they take, that they have not adjusted to American norms. For example, they are totally committed to heritage culture and language maintenance, almost with a zeal. Both groups also have an extremely favorable self-image, one that seems exaggerated. And they both clearly have negative images of all other ethnic groups, particularly hostile in the case of blacks. When compared with Polish Americans, their values, as measured with the Kluckhohn scale, reveal a much more fatalistic outlook on life, a desire to remain close to the nuclear family, and a strong emphasis on not expecting too much out of life. Judging from Rosen's work (Rosen, 1959; McClelland, 1961), the Polish values are more typically American which makes those of the Albanians and Arabs deviations from the American value norms. These un-American features of the perspectives of the Albanian and Arab parents seem to us to reflect a confusion regarding what they should do to accommodate to American life, possibly attributable to their more recent arrival.   For instance, the extreme pressure placed on the Albanian children to succeed in education and occupational career comes from parents whose overall value profile suggests anything but need achievement on their own part (see Rosen, 1959 and Rosen and D'Andrade, 1959).   Another example of confusion about American norms is the strong desire of the Arab parents to have Arabic utilized as an instructional medium in the public schools. Furthermore, both groups show a preference for sex-segregated classes, strictly not an American reflex.   Perhaps the clearest example of confusion about American norms is the negative, stereotyped categorization of other ethnic groups and the openly expressed disdain for black Americans.

The major conclusion, up to this point, is that our

examination of the feelings, attitudes and social
perceptions of these three ethnic immigrant groups has
revealed a common or shared appreciation for a
multicultural organization of American society over one
that promotes assimilation, and an equally strong
appreciation for having children become thoroughly
bilingual in English plus a heritage language. All three
groups support this form of bilingualism for all other
ethnic minorities, not only for their own children. But
our findings, so far, indicate that these shared
perspective do not bring the three groups together in terms
of intergroup attitudes and relationships. The Polish
American parents reveal a much more tolerant outlook on
other ethnic groups. This could be both a cause and a
consequence of their being the most successful ethnic group
in the community. It could also be a simple consequence of
having lived longer in America. Intergroup tensions exist
in the community, and judging from the attitude profiles
generated so far, the Albanian and Arab parents contribute
to these tensions, possibly because they lack knowledge of
American value norms on intergroup relations. There are,
however, other players to be brought into the total picture
before we can get a clear view of all that is happening in
this American center. In the next chapter we examine the
views of two other ethnic immigrant groups in the same
general setting.

Table 3.1

Responses of Ethnic Groups in Hamtramck
Regarding Assimilation and Culture Maintenance*

Culture Maintenance:

	Polish American Respondents	Arab American Respondents	Albanian American Respondents
Arguments Against			
All people living in America will not have a common base for understanding each other	2.81	3.62	3.72
There will be different languages and cultural standards throughout America	5.61	6.29	5.40
America will be divided into segregated units	2.84	2.71	3.10
Arguments For			
People will be allowed to express an important part of their identity	5.52	6.57	6.46
People will feel secure in their group identity, and this will make them open and sympathetic to other groups	5.84	4.95	6.51
The nation can keep the best that different cultural and racial groups have to offer	6.10	6.90	6.85

DISAGREE 1　2　3　4　5　6　7 AGREE
Definitely　　Neutral　　Definitely

Assimilation:

	Polish American Respondents	Arab American Respondents	Albanian American Respondents
Arguments For			
All people living in America will have a common base for understanding each other	3.45	4.10	3.97
The same language and cultural standards will exist for all	3.87	3.57	4.26
America will be unified and cohesive	3.50	4.19	4.64
Arguments Against			
People will be robbed of a very important part of their personal identity	4.74	6.76	5.92
People will have been forced to give up something valuable, and this will make them hostile toward others	4.52	6.71	6.41
The nation loses the best that different cultural and racial groups have to offer	4.94	6.85	6.51

DISAGREE 1　2　3　4　5　6　7 AGREE
Definitely　　Neutral　　Definitely

* Data analyzed by means of Kruskal-Wallis Chi Square. Connecting bars indicate statistical significance at one per cent level of confidence.

Table 3.2

Mean Scores for Ethnic Groups in Hamtramck
Regarding Retention of the Heritage Culture*

In your opinion, how far should your own group go in maintaining its culture and traditions?	Polish American Respondents	Arab American Respondents	Albanian American Respondents
1. Step A: Since our culture and traditions are not American, they should not be maintained.	3.16	1.50	2.31
2. Step B: Keep our own cultural styles of foods, dress, songs and dances.	6.61	6.57	6.51
3. Step C: Keep our own cultural values, such as how children should behave with parents, husbands with wives, dating practices, etc	6.10	6.45	6.56
4. Step D: Attend courses about our own cultural history and traditions, not in public schools but in church-run or community-run classes.	5.19	6.36	6.23
5. Step E: Have courses about our own cultural history and traditions taught in public schools.	4.81	6.60	6.10
6. Step F: Have equal time in schools spent on our own cultural history and traditions as on American history & traditions	4.71	5.07	5.18

DISAGREE 1____2____3____4____5____6____7 AGREE
          Definitely   Neutral   Definitely

---

* Data analyzed by means of Kruskal-Wallis Chi Square. Connecting bars indicate statistical significance at one per cent level of confidence.

Table 3.3

Mean Scores for Ethnic Groups in Hamtramck
Regarding the Maintenance of the Heritage Language*

In your opinion, how far should your own group go in using its its own language?	Polish American Respondents	Arab American Respondents	Albanian American Respondents
1. Step A: Cultural groups whose language is not Standard English should never use own language.	2.13	1.48	1.87
2. Step B: Use our own language for festival days, cultural songs, traditional stories, prayers and religious services.	5.87	6.91	6.87
3. Step C: Use our own language for speaking with older family members, like grandparents.	6.52	6.93	6.90
4. Step D: Use our own language for most or all speaking within the family.	5.77	6.74	6.87
5. Step E: Learn to read and write our own language not through school, but through church-run or community-run classes.	5.23	6.69	6.72
6. Step F: Use own language for part of the teaching and learning in public schools.	4.52	6.74	6.21
7. Step G: Give equal time in schools to the use of own language as to Standard English.	3.81	5.05	3.69

DISAGREE 1_____2_____3_____4_____5_____6_____7 AGREE

Definitely   Neutral   Definitely

---

* Data analyzed by means of Kruskal-Wallis Chi Square. Connecting bars indicate statistical significance at one per cent level of confidence.

Table 3.4

Mean Scores Regarding the Consequences of Bilingualism*

Would they:	Polish American Respondents			Arab American Respondents			Albanian American Respondents		
	If your son/ daughter were bilingual...	If your son/ daughter spoke only Polish...	If your son/ daughter spoke only English...	If your son/ daughter were bilingual...	If your son/ daughter spoke only Arabic...	If your son/ daughter spoke only English	If your son/ daughter were only bilingual	If your son/ daughter spoke only Albanian	If your son/ daughter spoke only English
1. Feel accepted in America?	6.42	3.77	6.26	6.86	2.36	4.95	6.90	3.21	6.92
2. Feel a sense of pride?	6.13	4.45	5.71	6.86	4.52	4.48	6.88	2.60	3.18
3. Make their parents happy?	6.36	4.39	5.36	6.93	4.83	4.69	7.00	2.00	2.23
4. Feel open and relaxed with others?	6.13	2.90	6.00	6.76	2.14	4.31	6.68	2.64	4.87
5. Bring status and respect to their group?	6.19	4.45	5.65	6.74	5.38	4.48	6.72	2.67	2.92
6. Stand out as different?	2.74	4.61	2.36	2.41	4.29	3.31	4.03	4.33	3.33
7. Be treated like second-class citizens?	1.52	3.68	4.77	2.69	3.86	3.41	2.44	5.10	3.00
8. Get good marks in school?	5.26	3.45	4.77	6.88	1.79	4.12	6.00	2.03	4.90
9. Have a chance for certain jobs others can't get?	5.71	2.97	4.55	6.76	2.48	4.62	6.00	2.18	4.77
10. Be sympathetic to people?	4.74	4.03	4.39	5.67	5.07	5.05	6.08	3.51	4.74
11. Show intelligence?	5.74	4.65	5.19	4.60	2.60	2.60	6.59	2.39	4.59

NO 1___2___3___4___5___6___7 YES
Definitely   Neutral   Definitely

---

* Data analyzed by means of Wilcoxon sign-ranks test. Connecting bars indicate statistical significance at one per cent level of confidence.

Table 3.5

Mean Attribution Ratings of Own Group and Other Groups in Hamtramck[a]

How... are...	Polish American Respondents				Arab American Respondents				Albanian American Respondents			
	most Polish Americans	most Arab Americans	most Albanian Americans	most black Americans	most Polish Americans	most Arab Americans	most Albanian Americans	most black Americans	most Polish Americans	most Arab Americans	most Albanian Americans	most black Americans
1. hardworking	6.16	4.80	4.97	3.87	4.21	5.12	4.05	2.86	5.08	4.70	5.23	3.10
2. aggressive or violent	3.32	5.03	5.87	5.43	3.28	1.76	3.74	4.71	2.95	3.40	2.98	5.78
3. American	5.10	3.43	3.47	4.97	4.08	3.27	4.18	4.85	5.35	3.36	4.43	3.60
4. likely to stick together as a group	6.10	6.20	6.10	6.20	5.21	5.60	5.13	5.26	5.48	5.08	5.92	4.65
5. powerful	5.13	5.13	5.17	5.27	4.10	3.69	3.80	4.43	5.18	3.58	3.90	3.33
6. similar to me	5.45	2.90	3.03	3.00	3.36	5.52	3.97	2.10	4.45	3.35	6.59	1.85
7. intelligent at school	6.00	4.43	4.20	4.13	4.03	4.98	3.74	2.45	5.20	4.03	5.20	2.63
8. smart with practical things	6.16	4.87	4.80	4.43	4.18	4.83	3.82	2.41	5.45	4.10	5.28	3.00
9. trustworthy	5.97	4.17	4.20	4.07	3.69	5.76	3.41	1.64	4.59	4.43	6.26	2.28
10. law-abiding (good citizen)	6.13	4.27	4.00	3.70	4.18	5.93	3.90	2.17	5.55	4.18	5.15	2.63
11. unfairly treated	3.48	3.63	3.47	3.57	3.64	4.12	3.74	4.00	2.73	3.08	2.72	5.00
12. likable	6.13	4.07	3.09	4.37	3.82	4.60	3.77	2.83	4.40	3.42	5.84	2.51

```
NOT AT ALL  1     2     3     4     5     6     7  VERY
         Definitely      Neutral      Definitely
```

[a] Data analyzed by means of Wilcoxon sign-ranks test. Connecting bars indicate statistical significance at one per cent level of confidence.

79

Table 3.6

Mean Social Distance Ratings in Hamtramck*

How willing are you personally to accept these people?	Polish American Respondents				Arab American Respondents				Albanian American Respondents			
	most Polish Americans	most Arab Americans	most Albanian Americans	most Black Americans	most Polish Americans	most Arab Americans	most Albanian Americans	most Black Americans	most Polish Americans	most Arab Americans	most Albanian Americans	most Black Americans
1. As a family member through marriage?	6.68	3.00	3.13	2.16	1.02	6.93	1.19	1.02	2.63	1.23	7.00	1.00
2. As a close personal friend?	6.77	4.36	4.45	4.10	2.76	6.48	2.64	2.36	4.73	3.03	6.90	2.00
3. As a close neighbor in my neighborhood or apartment building?	6.55	3.90	4.16	3.58	2.67	6.48	2.69	2.33	4.85	2.80	6.77	1.78
4. As a co-worker or or partner at work?	6.52	4.65	4.68	4.84	2.17	5.71	2.17	1.98	4.93	3.20	6.62	3.20
5. As a citizen of the U.S.A.?	6.77	5.03	4.81	5.39	6.79	6.86	6.76	6.76	5.48	4.35	5.60	3.35

```
NOT AT ALL   1     2     3     4     5     6     7   VERY
          Definitely        Neutral         Definitely
```

* Data analyzed by means of Wilcoxon sign-ranks test. Connecting bars indicate statistical significance at one percent level of confidence.

80

Table 3.7

Mean Scores for Ethnic Groups in Hamtramck
Regarding Basic Values*

	Polish American Respondents	Arab American Respondents	Albanian American Respondents
1. All a person should want out of life in the way of a career is a secure, not too.....	3.84	4.83	5.30
2. When people are born, the success they are going to have is already in the cards....	2.68	5.19	4.38
3. The secret of happiness is not expecting too much out of life and being content...	3.68	4.19	5.23
4. Nothing is worth the sacrifice of moving away from one's parents.....	3.84	6.88	5.45
5. The best kind of job to have is one where you are part of an organization.....	3.81	5.91	3.78
6. Planning only makes a person unhappy since your plans hardly ever.....	3.97	3.00	5.45
7. Nowadays with world conditions the way they are, the wise person lives for today......	2.87	2.31	2.23

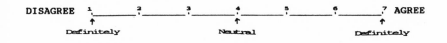

DISAGREE 1_____2_____3_____4_____5_____6_____7 AGREE
              ↑   ↑   ↑
          Definitely   Neutral   Definitely

---

* Data analyzed by means of Kruskal-Wallis Chi Square. Connecting bars indicate statistical significance at one percent level of confidence.

81

Table 3.8

Mean Scores for Ethnic Groups in Hamtramck
Regarding Education*

	Polish American Respondents	Arab American Respondents	Albanian American Respondents
1. The future is bright for young people.	5.16	5.81	5.50
2. Education is more important today than past.	6.65	6.91	6.00
3. Education would be better if boys and girls separated.	2.84	6.07	5.10
4. Schools should not have dances.	2.61	5.73	5.13
5. Schools should have a racial mix of children.	5.84	5.66	5.55
6. Children should be taught more discipline in school.	6.55	6.78	7.00
7. Teachers are not as devoted to students as in past.	4.42	4.10	6.20
8. High school graduation isn't enough.	5.94	6.55	6.80
9. Students aren't as interested in learning as in past.	4.55	4.98	6.60
10. Parents don't show enough interest in children's education.	4.74	3.38	6.10
11. Schools don't give enough say to parents.	4.61	3.71	6.43

DISAGREE 1_____2_____3_____4_____5_____6_____7 AGREE

Definitely   Neutral   Definitely

_____

* Data analyzed by means of Kruskal-Wallis Chi Square.
Connecting bars indicate statistical significance at one
percent level of confidence.

82

Table 3.9

Mean Scores for Ethnic Group in Hamtramck
Regarding School Subjects*

	Polish American Respondents	Arab American Respondents	Albanian American Respondents
1. English language arts	6.77	6.48	6.98
2. Language arts for own language	5.43	6.81	6.50
3. Language arts for another language	5.32	5.62	6.10
4. Mathematics	6.81	7.00	6.93
5. Science	6.58	7.00	6.90
6. Computers	6.52	6.98	6.73
7. American history	6.07	7.00	6.50
8. History of own group	5.71	6.83	6.60
9. History of other groups	5.23	6.62	5.63
10. Music	5.55	6.31	6.08
11. Physical education	5.97	6.86	6.30
12. Hygiene and health	6.32	6.98	6.80
13. Sex education	5.40	2.55	2.98
14. Practical/technical training	6.07	6.91	6.08

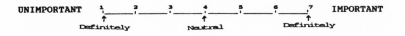

UNIMPORTANT 1___2___3___4___5___6___7 IMPORTANT
              ↑   ↑   ↑
          Definitely   Neutral   Definitely

* Data analyzed by means of Kruskal-Wallis Chi Square. Connecting bars indicate statistical significance at one percent level of confidence.

83

Table 3.10

Mean Scores for Ethnic Groups in Hamtramck
Regarding the Desirability and Likelihood of Employment Prospects[*]

	How happy would you be if your son/daughter became.........			What are the chances of your son/daughter becoming.....		
	Polish American Respondents	Arab American Respondents	Albanian American Respondents	Polish American Respondents	Arab American Respondents	Albanian American Respondents
1. a lawyer, a doctor, a director of a large company, etc. (a major professional position)?	6.71	6.79	7.00	4.94	4.38	5.32
2. an owner of a small business, small restaurant, a bookkeeper, (a minor professional position)?	6.29	6.19	5.83	5.10	5.10	5.38
3. a machinist, roofer, plumber, nurse, secretary (a skilled worker position)?	6.26	5.36	4.33	5.55	5.14	4.10
4. a road repair man, gas station attendant, a file clerk (a semi skilled worker position)?	5.10	4.02	2.55	4.90	5.48	2.63
5. a daily laborer in a factory or on a construction project, a house cleaner (an unskilled worker position)?	1.33	2.00	1.33	4.65	5.86	1.73

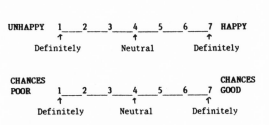

```
UNHAPPY   1____2____3____4____5____6____7  HAPPY
          ↑              ↑              ↑
       Definitely     Neutral      Definitely


CHANCES                                    CHANCES
POOR      1____2____3____4____5____6____7   GOOD
          ↑              ↑              ↑
       Definitely     Neutral      Definitely
```

* Data analyzed by means of Kruskal-Wallis Chi Square. Connecting bars indicate statistical significance at one percent level of confidence.

4

Ethnic Immigrant Groups in Pontiac: Mexican and Puerto Rican Americans

Situated twenty miles north of Hamtramck and still in the greater Detroit area, the city of Pontiac gives the impression of being just as ethnic as Hamtramck even though the languages and ethnic groups one encounters, with the exception of a large black population, are entirely different. People with Polish, Albanian or Arabic ancestry would be rare or nonexistent in Pontiac just as those with Puerto Rican and Mexican American ancestry, forming sizable groups in Pontiac, would be statistically rare in Hamtramck. As already mentioned, Pontiac also has two prominent groups of whites, representing two sharply contrasting social class levels. There is also a small but growing group of Vietnamese immigrants or refugees. Thus, from an ethnolinguistic point of view, Pontiac and Hamtramck seem worlds rather than miles apart. Indeed, blacks constitute the only large ethnic group encountered in both communities.

Most important for our study, Pontiac offered us the opportunity to   extend our investigation, not only with a different ethnic group, but in   particular with two Hispanic groups--Mexican Americans and Puerto Rican Americans--the two groups that have become so large that their presence has   made the whole issue of cultural and linguistic diversity the salient topic   it actually is in the United States.   Consequently, the central question we deal with   in this chapter is: Will these major Hispanic ethnic groups, through their   reactions to our interview instruments, throw a different light   or a brighter light on multiculturalism in America?

MEXICAN AMERICAN PERSPECTIVES

Heritage Culture Maintenance versus Assimilation

There is no ambiguity about the position taken by our sample of Mexican   American parents on the debate over heritage culture maintenance versus   assimilation.   Their responses, presented in Figure 4.1 make it crystal clear that they strongly favor the culture maintenance option. The mean score for   the Mexican American parents as a group is 6.05 on the seven-point scale and the   parent-to-parent variability is extremely small.

When asked to consider the arguments for and against culture maintenance,   the Mexican American parents reveal a consistent viewpoint (see Table 4.1).   In their eyes, allowing ethnic groups to maintain their culture means allowing them to express an   important part of their identity.   It also means   that the nation as a whole can keep the best that different groups have to   offer, that all groups will feel secure in their group identities, and that   this in turn will make them open and sympathetic to others.   Mexican American   parents do not feel that a policy of culture maintenance would divide America   into segregated units or that there would no longer be a common base for   intergroup understanding.   They do recognize, however, that maintenance would   mean that a variety of differing cultural standards would be evident   throughout the nation.

When asked to consider the consequences of assimilation (Table 4.1), they   show the consistency of their stand by rating that assimilation would rob   people

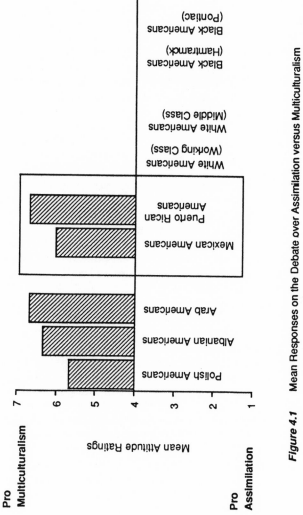

Figure 4.1   Mean Responses on the Debate over Assimilation versus Multiculturalism

of a very important part of their personal identities, that people would feel more hostile toward other ethnic groups and that the nation would lose the best that different cultural and racial groups have to offer. Their overall sentiments are not only consistent, but also strong and clear.

Heritage Culture and Language: How Much is Desirable?
When considering ways to keep their culture alive, the Mexican American parents feel that they should not only maintain their own cultural styles of food, dress, songs, and dances, but also maintain cultural values, for example, how children should behave with parents, how they should deal with dating, etc. (see Table 4.2).   They endorse the idea of having church or community-run classes to teach their own cultural history, but favor, even more, having their own cultural history courses taught in public schools. To a lesser extent, they even support the notion of equal school time for their own cultural history as for American history and traditions.

Supplemental analyses also indicated that Mexican American parents are equally supportive of other ethnic groups in the community who might also want to maintain their cultures and traditions.

On the question of using and maintaining the heritage language (Table 4.3), the Mexican American parents feel that it is appropriate not only to speak Spanish within the family, and for festival days and religious services, but also that Spanish be used as the medium of instruction for part of the teaching in public schools and/or in community-run classes. They even support, although less strongly, the idea of having half of the public school teaching conducted through Spanish and half through English. Consistently, they extend the same support for this form of bilingual education to other ethnolinguistic groups, and in general indicate that the modes of keeping Spanish alive in their families should be available to other ethnic groups with their own languages.

Maintenance and Use of the Heritage Language: Mexican American Parents

The Choice: Heritage Language, English, Bilingualism.
What would be the consequences for Mexican American children if they developed fluency in English only, as

opposed to fluency in Spanish only, or fluently in both English and Spanish?   Our sample of Mexican American parents have a clear and consistent attitude on this issue as well (see Table   4.4).   For them, the greatest advantages fall to the bilingual child. Being bilingual in Spanish and English would help their children feel more accepted   in America, feel a greater sense of pride about themselves, bring more status and respect to their group, feel   more   open   and   relaxed   with   others   in   the neighborhood, and compete more effectively for jobs, than would be the case   for either the English only or the Spanish only alternative.   It would also   make parents happiest.   Nonetheless, they also endorse the English only alternative, but less enthusiastically.   They would be unmistakably least satisfied with the Spanish only option, for it is perceived as a major   handicap. Without English, their children would not have access to jobs, would not be accepted in America, would not bring status and respect to their group, and would not be considered intelligent.

Mexican American Attitudes Towards Own and Other Ethnic Groups

Attitudes.   The generosity extended to other groups on the issue of culture and language maintenance is not reflected in the attitudes Mexican American parents express towards other groups.   In fact, they present a very   favorable view of their own group, seeing Mexican Americans as the most hardworking, trustworthy, law abiding, likable group of all those considered, and   also the smartest with practical things (see Table 4.5).   However, this   value attributed to own group does not generalize to others.   Blacks are seen   as being not hardworking, trustworthy, law abiding and not even unfairly   treated.   Instead, blacks are perceived as particularly violent and   aggressive, powerful, and likely to stick together as a group.   In no way are they rated as "similar".

Of special interest are the attitudes of Mexican American parents towards Puerto Ricans.   Their views of Puerto Ricans are at best neutral, with no   expressed sentiment for a pan-Hispanic closeness.   For instance, although Puerto Ricans are rated much as Mexican Americans themselves, (i.e. as being not "American" and as being less powerful than black or white Americans), the similarity seems to stop there.   Puerto Ricans are not rated as "similar", and they are considered much less likable, trustworthy, hardworking, determined to succeed, law-abiding, intelligent and smart, and more aggressive and violent than Mexican Americans. Similarly, White Americans are viewed as less hardworking, trustworthy, and likable, no more intelligent or smart, but more powerful and, of course, much more American. Overall, the profile is basically one of own-group-centered ethnocentricity with sharp invidious contrasts drawn between their own group and each of the other ethnic groups in the country. Thus, through their network of attitudes, Mexican American parents in Pontiac see their group as standing apart from other groups, even from Puerto Ricans.

Social Distance. A similar pattern emerges in the social distance ratings. Mexican Americans would be more willing to accept white Americans and Puerto Ricans at the most intimate step of social distance (i.e., as a family member through marriage) than black Americans (see Table 4.6), but they would not be overjoyed by these prospects since the mean for the acceptability of white Americans as family members is only 4.65 and for Puerto Ricans, 4.30. Clearly, the preference is for own-group marriage partners. They are more accepting of other ethnic groups at the other social distance levels, as close personal friends, neighbors, co-workers, and co-citizens. But even outside the marriage domain, there are definite differences in acceptability registered in their ratings. They even keep Puerto Rican Americans at a discernible social distance at each step, except for citizenship.

THE PERSPECTIVES OF PUERTO RICAN AMERICAN PARENTS

Heritage Culture Maintenance versus Assimilation

The Puerto Rican group takes a very strong position, even more extreme than the Mexican Americans, in favor of ethnic groups maintaining distinctive cultural ways of life when they come to the United States (see Figure 4.1). The reasons they give for the position taken are consistent and basically similar to those of the Mexican Americans (Table 4.1). Through cultural maintenance people would be better able to express an important part of their identity and that this in turn would make them more open and sympathetic to other ethnic groups; the nation would be

better off   because different cultural and racial groups
would be able to express the best attributes each has to
offer.   At the same time, they acknowledge that
maintenance would mean a diversification of languages and
cultural standards   in the nation, but they apparently do
not view this diversity as a potential   problem, because
they argue that America would not be divided into
segregated units if heritage cultures were given a chance
to flourish.

     The consistency of their views is clear in their
responses to questions   about the consequences of an
assimilation policy.   In that case, they argue,   people
would be deprived of an important part of their identity,
would be made more hostile towards other groups, and the
nation would subsequently lose out   on the best that
different ethnic groups have to offer.   Furthermore, they
do   not feel that America would be any more unified and
cohesive if various   groups did give up their traditional
ways.   There is, therefore, a strong   concensus of views
favoring the multicultural alternative over assimilation,
and the concensus includes all ethnic immigrant groups
studied--both Hispanic groups in Pontiac and the Arab,
Albanian and Polish groups in Hamtramck.

Heritage Culture and Language: How Much is Desirable? The
Puerto Rican parents are the most emphatic in their
endorsement of various steps that   should be taken to
maintain heritage cultures in America (Table 4.2). They
feel that their styles of foods, dress, songs and dances,
as well as their own cultural values should be maintained.
Further, they believe that Puerto Rican history should not
be taught in community or church-run classes, but   rather
in the public school system itself.   They are even willing
to endorse equal proportions of time for the teaching of
Puerto Rican history as for American history.   In this
respect they are the most extreme of all groups
interviewed.   Furthermore, they endorse the public school
teaching of other groups' cultural history as well as
their own group (see Table 4.2).   In other words, their
feelings about culture maintenance clearly extend to other
groups besides their own.

     Similarly, in terms of language maintenance (Table
4.2), they feel that Spanish should be used within the
home, and that the public system should allow equal time
for instruction through Spanish as through English.   No
other group in Pontiac feels quite so strongly about

endorsing this degree of bilingual instruction. As noted, the Mexican American group feels that it would be just as appropriate to learn to read and write Spanish in out-of-school, community run classes as in the public schools whereas the Puerto Rican parents focus particularly on public schools for heritage language development. In fact, they do not endorse as strongly as other Pontiac groups do the use of heritage languages for festival days, religious services, or for speaking with older family members, suggesting that such activities, along with a reliance on community-run classes, might promote a mere token-type culture maintenance.

Maintenance and Use of the Heritage Language: Puerto Rican Parents

The Choice: Heritage Language, English, Bilingualism. As was the case in Hamtramck, groups in Pontiac strongly support the notion of bilingualism, and the Puerto Rican Americans stand out as particularly favorable (Table 4.4). There is in fact a strong consensus in our sample of Puerto Rican parents to the effect that their children, if fluently bilingual in English and Spanish, would not only please their parents but also feel a sense of pride about who they are, feel accepted in America, have chances for certain jobs that others can't get, feel open and relaxed with others in the neighborhood, and bring status and respect to the Puerto Rican American community as a whole. Being bilingual would not make them stand out as different or make them feel like second-class citizens.

The Puerto Rican parents also endorse the option of their children becoming fluent in English only, although that would make the parents less happy than the bilingual alternative. They also feel that their children would not have as much pride in themselves if they commanded English only. On the other hand, they do not believe that speaking Spanish only would give children this sense of pride. It would instead put them in jeopardy: they would not feel accepted in America, not feel comfortable in the neighborhood, would stand out as different, and they would be hindered in both school and employment opportunities.

Puerto Rican Attitudes Towards Own and Other Ethnic Groups

Attitudes. The Puerto Rican parents as a group present a pattern of intergroup attitudes much like that of the Mexican Americans which means that it too reflects a disquieting ethnocentrism and distancing of own group from other groups.   Still there are subtle differences in the attitude networks of the two Hispanic groups. The Puerto Rican parents describe their own group as being powerful, likable, intelligent at school, smart with practical things, determined to succeed, intelligent, and law-abiding. Their favorable self-ratings are in fact the most extreme of all groups interviewed (see Table 4.5).

However, sharp contrasts are drawn with each of the other community groups. No other group is rated as at all similar to themselves. Blacks are seen as untrustworthy, not hardworking, and very aggressive or violent.   Whites also are rated only marginally in terms of trustworthy and hardworking, and as significantly less intelligent and smart than Puerto Ricans themselves. Mexican Americans are also perceived as reliably less trustworthy, law abiding, and likable than Puerto Ricans, no different than black Americans in these characteristics.   Mexican Americans are no more "similar" to Puerto Ricans than are black or white Americans. Furthermore, a very sharp contrast is drawn on the issue of "American": Puerto Ricans see themselves as being as American as are black and white Americans whereas Mexican Americans are decidedly not American.   Recall that the reciprocal view of Mexican American parents was substantially different: they saw both their own group and the Puerto Rican as being not American. Finally, the Puerto Rican parents see two groups as having most "power"--their own group and blacks, both having reliably more power than Mexican Americans or white Americans.

Social Distance. Regardless of the attributions they assign to the other ethnic groups in Pontiac and the ethnocentrism that is suggested, the Puerto Rican Americans differ from the Mexican Americans by being very willing to accept members from all the other groups in Pontiac (whites, blacks, and Mexican Americans) as close personal friends, neighbors, co-workers and co-citizens (Table 4.6).   In fact, they are the most charitable group in Pontiac in their degree of acceptance of other groups.

One wonders though how deep the acceptance goes if, for example, acceptable close personal friendships with blacks or Mexican Americans are based on the ethnocentric attitudes this group of parents expressed towards these same ethnic groups. The one area where they do keep a distance however is on the issue of family membership through marriage. As a group, they would be less than delighted if their family members married either Mexican or white Americans and they find marriage with Black Americans definitely unacceptable.

Parental Value Orientations and Expectations for Children: Hispanic Perspective

As in the Hamtramck study, we have found two different ethnolinguistic immigrant groups in Pontiac who express a very determined desire to keep their distinctive cultures and their heritage language alive in the United States setting. We have also found both Hispanic groups show a strong ethnic pride, but both have strong ethnocentric networks of attitudes towards other ethnic groups in the community. Here we explore, through an examination of their values and the expectations they have for their children, whether there are other, perhaps more fundamental, dimensions of perception that might throw light on how these two Hispanic groups accommodate to the community at large.

Value Orientations

The group comparisons on the Kluckhohn scale of values are presented in Table 4.7. What we note first is that, rather than value clashes, there is a good deal of value overlap between the two Hispanic groups with no signs of sharply contrasting profiles or major deviations from American norms, as was the case with two of the ethnic immigrant groups in Hamtramck. Both groups reject the ideas that fate controls one's success, that one shouldn't expect too much from life, and that one should reside close to one's parents. Thus, both groups reflect the expected American values, especially achievement through personal endeavors. Nonetheless, on one item of the scale, both groups endorse a position that is discordant with an accepted American value: both support fairly strongly the idea that one should seek security and ease in a career.

Similarly, neither group rejects the idea of living for today.   Overall, then, although particular values run somewhat counter to an American   achievement-oriented pattern, both the Mexican and the Puerto Rican American parents present a common profile of values that is close to that expected of working class Americans.

Attitudes Towards Public Education

Because all parents interviewed have one or more children in school and because public schools are the major arena for inter-ethnic group contact, we surveyed in detail their views on education (Table 4.8). With respect to the importance of education, both groups agree that it is "very important" and they even indicate that high school graduation is no guarantee for employment. The Puerto Rican parents especially are emphatic on this last point (M = 6.82).

With regard to the structure of public schools, both Mexican and Puerto Rican American parents endorse the full integration of children from different ethnic and racial backgrounds in school. Both groups also strongly favor sexually integrated classes, and the encouragement of co-educational social events. Both groups also agree that children should be "taught more discipline" in schools.

The two groups agree as well that teachers today are not as devoted to students as they used to be, that students themselves are not as interested in learning, and that parents are not sufficiently involved in their children's education. It is of interest that the feeling of a generalized lack of involvement in education and the need for more discipline are common themes for all immigrant groups surveyed. As we will see in later chapters, this concern is more pronounced for new Americans than it is for the more established white and black host groups who may take public education for granted or simply have lower expectations about public education. We presume it represents a particularly serious concern for ethnic immigrant parents perhaps because they may feel inadequate to discuss with teachers or otherwise get involved themselves and thus may feel negligent on this count.

Another real possibility is that ethnic immigrants soon learn that schools are run by particular groups only. In Hamtramck, the administration is almost exclusively drawn from the Polish American community and in Pontiac from the white and black communities. The point is that Albanian, Arab and the two Hispanic groups may be more critical of the education system because they have little say in its functioning.

With respect the relative importance of various subject matters, both the Puerto Rican and Mexican American parents believe that mathematics, science, computer technology, and English language arts are very important subject matters for their children (Table 4.9), more so than music, sex education, and courses in other groups' histories (other than their own and American). Overall, there is a general agreement about the curriculum makeup, with slight differences in emphasis, and both groups are basically similar in their judgments to other parental groups whether immigrants or established Americans.

Education and the World of Work.   As would be expected, both parental groups would feel progressively more satisfied the higher the occupational level their children might ultimately achieve (Table 4.10). Thus they would be happiest were their children to become doctors or lawyers and least content if they were only able to become unskilled workers. What is more instructive is the degree of discontent each group expresses for the possibility of a low occupational outcome: Puerto Rican Americans would be quite upset by such an eventuality, noticeably more upset than the Mexican American parents who, reflecting a quite different outlook on unemployment, would be content if their children find work of any sort.

This group difference is apparent as well in their estimates of the likelihood of their children's future occupational level (see Table 4.10). The Puerto Rican parents have generally higher occupational expectations for their children than the Mexican American parents who are perhaps more realistic about the probabilities that their children may eventually only find work at the skilled or even unskilled worker levels. The importance of these differences lies in the consequences each outlook might have on the children implicated: if the Mexican American parents resign themselves to harsh realities about work, might this resignation promote its own self fulfillment? If the Puerto Rican parents don't face the realities of large numbers of minority group members being unemployed in the U.S., might their optimism promote frustration directed towards self and resentment directed towards the society as a whole? In either case, Mexican Americans in particular but Puerto Ricans as well face a reality of becoming permanent members of America's "underclass", as Pachon and Moore explain (1981). The probabilities are high that second and third generation members of these groups will fall into the "secondary labor market, characterized by relatively dead-end jobs that pay low wages, offer little security, and provide limited chances for economic advancement" (Pachon & Moore, 1981, p. 119).

In summary, then, the supplemental comparisons made on our two Hispanic groups show them to be generally in agreement on basic values, on their views of schooling and how it should be conducted, and on occupational prospects for their children. The more subtle contrasts that turned up between Mexican and Puerto Rican Americans are intrinsically informative, but for the American society at large, these two groups are not making outlandish demands and their basic value orientations seem to be in line with American norms.

We say "seem to be" because now it becomes evident that we need to shift our focus to the more established Americans, the "host" groups who are clearly not uninterested, passive observers of these more recent arrivals.   They are the norm setters, or at least most theorists would expect them to be. One thing is certain: the more established Americans are in daily interaction with and in many respects in competition with these ethnic newcomers, not only in the world of work, but also in the world of assimilation. They are the ones who are in positions to show newcomers what it is to be American. Accordingly, in the next chapter we add two important new groups to our analysis--two social class groups of white, established Americans whose views on assimilation and multiculturalism are critical.

Table 4.1

Responses of Ethnic Groups in Pontiac Regarding Assimilation and Culture Maintenance*

Culture Maintenance Arguments:

	Mexican American Respondents	Puerto Rican American Respondents
Arguments Against		
All people living in America will not have a common base for understanding each other	2.25	2.65
There will be different languages and cultural standards throughout America	4.78 ⎦	6.23 ⎦
America will be divided into segregated units	2.39	1.80
Arguments For		
People will be allowed to express an important part of their identity	6.05	6.90
People will feel secure in their group identity, and this will make them open and sympathetic to other groups	5.53 ⎦	6.88 ⎦
The nation can keep the best that different cultural and racial groups have to offer	5.80	6.68

Assimilation Arguments:

	Mexican American Respondents	Puerto Rican American Respondents
Arguments For		
All people living in America will have a common base for understanding each other	2.58	3.03
The same language and cultural standards will exist for all Americans	3.46	3.75
America will be unified and cohesive	2.58	2.28
Arguments Against		
People will be robbed of a very important part of their personal identity	6.05	6.60
People will have been forced to give up something valuable, and this will make them hostile toward others	5.30	5.98
The nation loses the best that different cultural and racial groups have to offer	5.78	5.88

```
DISAGREE   1 _____ 2 ___ 3 ___ 4 ___ 5 ___ 6 ___ 7   AGREE
         Definitely            Neutral          Definitely
```

* Data analyzed by means of Kruskal-Wallis Chi Square. Connecting bars indicate statistical significance at one percent level of confidence.

Table 4.2

Mean Scores for Ethnic Groups in Pontiac
Regarding Retention of the Heritage Culture*

In your opinion, how far should your own group go in maintaining its culture and traditions?	Mexican American Respondents	Puerto Rican American Respondents
1. Step A: Since our culture and traditions are not American, they should not be maintained.	2.15	1.08
2. Step B: Keep our own cultural styles of foods, dress, songs and dances.	6.08	6.83
3. Step C: Keep our own cultural values, such as how children should behave with parents, husbands with wives, dating practices, etc	6.38	6.73
4. Step D: Attend courses about our own cultural history and traditions, not in public schools but in church run or community run classes.	5.53	2.35
5. Step E: Have courses about our own cultural history and traditions taught in public schools.	5.65	6.83
6. Step F: Have equal time in schools spent on our own cultural history and traditions as on American history & traditions	5.36	6.63

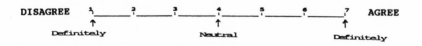

DISAGREE 1_____2_____3_____4_____5_____6_____7 AGREE
          ↑   ↑   ↑
      Definitely   Neutral   Definitely

---

* Data analyzed by means of Kruskal-Wallis Chi Square. Connecting
  bars indicate statistical significance at one percent level of
  confidence.

Table 4.3

Mean Scores for Ethnic Groups in Pontiac
Regarding the Maintenance of the Heritage Language*

In your opinion, how far should your own group go in using its its own language?	Mexican American Respondents	Puerto Rican American Respondents
1. Step A: Cultural groups whose language is not Standard English should never use own language.	1.56	1.10
2. Step B: Use our own language for festival days, cultural songs, traditional stories, prayers, and religious services,	6.55	4.95
3. Step C: Use our own language for speaking with older family members, like grandparents.	6.58	4.70
4. Step D: Use our own language for most or all speaking within the family.	6.03	5.78
5. Step E: Learn to read and write our own language not through school, but through church-run or community-run classes.	5.43	3.05
6. Step F: Use own language for part of the teaching and learning in public schools.	5.55	6.63
7. Step G: Give equal time in schools to the use of own language as to Standard English.	5.05	6.48

DISAGREE   1____2____3____4____5____6____7   AGREE
           Definitely   Neutral   Definitely

---

* Data analyzed by means of Kruskal-Wallis Chi Square. Connecting
  bars indicate statistical significance at one percent level of
  confidence.

Table 4.4

Mean Scores Regarding the Consequences of Bilingualism*

Would they:	Mexican American Respondents			Puerto Rican American Respondents		
	If your son/ daughter were bilingual...	If your son/ daughter spoke only Spanish..	If your son/ daughter spoke only English	If your son/ daughter were only bilingual	If your son/ daughter spoke only Spanish..	If your son/ daughter spoke only English..
1. feel accepted in America?	6.85	3.43	6.60	6.93	2.60	6.90
2. feel a sense of pride?	6.55	3.98	5.20	7.00	2.53	5.30
3. make their parents happy?	6.85	3.85	4.73	7.00	3.15	3.08
4. feel open and relaxed with others?	6.50	3.03	5.95	6.88	2.23	6.55
5. bring status and respect to their group?	6.18	3.48	4.73	6.85	5.63	3.05
6. stand out as different?	4.35	3.83	3.38	3.38	5.28	1.28
7. be treated like second class citizens?	2.70	4.78	2.93	3.13	5.23	1.93
8. get good marks in school?	5.88	2.38	4.88	6.35	1.80	6.68
9. have a chance for certain jobs others can't get?	6.50	2.80	4.85	6.90	1.78	6.63
10. be sympathetic to people from different groups?	5.73	4.05	5.08	6.55	5.33	6.53
11. show intelligence?	5.38	3.05	4.40	6.73	3.95	6.43

DISAGREE 1____2____3____4____5____6____7 AGREE
          Definitely   Neutral   Definitely

* Data analyzed by means of Wilcoxon sign-ranks test. Connecting bars indicate statistical significance at one per cent level of confidence.

101

Table 4.5

Mean Attribution Ratings of Own Group and Other Groups in Pontiac*

How ...... are	Mexican American Respondents				Puerto Rican American Respondents			
	Puerto Rican Americans most	Mexican Americans most	Black Americans most	White Americans most	Puerto Rican Americans most	Mexican Americans most	Black Americans most	White Americans most
1. hardworking	4.54	6.18	3.62	4.74	5.78	5.19	3.54	4.46
2. aggressive or violent	4.74	4.13	5.67	3.46	5.10	5.53	6.21	4.89
3. American	3.40	3.57	4.55	6.51	6.73	2.68	6.65	7.00
4. likely to stick together as a group	5.84	5.98	6.50	5.58	6.98	6.74	6.92	6.85
5. powerful	4.35	4.83	5.83	6.15	6.40	5.76	6.33	5.95
6. similar to me	3.35	6.27	1.90	2.38	5.95	1.87	1.51	1.92
7. intelligent at school	4.10	5.13	4.66	5.32	6.13	5.46	5.50	5.72
8. smart with practical things	4.81	5.74	4.27	5.44	6.35	5.94	5.33	5.92
9. trustworthy	4.18	5.85	3.23	3.93	5.45	3.97	3.51	4.00
10. law-abiding (good citizen)	4.49	5.67	3.37	5.26	6.18	5.08	4.50	5.03
11. unfairly treated	3.95	4.20	3.67	3.35	6.10	5.54	5.47	2.29
12. likable	4.95	5.70	4.38	4.78	6.43	5.41	4.79	4.92
13. determined to succeed	4.58	5.68	5.26	5.82	6.40	6.06	5.81	6.05

NOT AT ALL 1 2 3 4 5 6 7 VERY
Definitely   Neutral   Definitely

* Data analyzed by means of Wilcoxon sign-ranks test. Connecting bars indicate statistical significance at one percent level of confidence.

Table 4.6

Mean Social Distance Ratings in Pontiac*

How willing are you personally to accept these people?	Mexican American Respondents				Puerto Rican American Respondents			
	most Puerto Rican Americans	most Mexican Americans	most Black Americans	most White Americans	most Puerto Rican Americans	most Mexican Americans	most Black Americans	most White Americans
1. As a family member through marriage?	4.30	6.45	2.48	4.65	6.68	4.83	3.53	4.65
2. As a close personal friend?	5.95	6.48	5.23	5.53	6.83	6.70	6.58	6.60
3. As a close neighbor in my neighborhood or apartment building?	5.80	6.45	5.20	5.78	6.90	6.80	6.68	6.80
4. As a co-worker or partner at work?	5.88	6.53	5.43	5.73	6.90	6.80	6.63	6.80
5. As a citizen of the U.S.A.?	6.25	6.60	6.38	6.55	6.93	6.75	6.70	6.83

NOT AT ALL 1 2 3 4 5 6 7 **VERY**

Definitely   Neutral   Definitely

---

* Data analyzed by means of Wilcoxon sign-ranks test. Connecting bars indicate statistical significance at one percent level of confidence.

103

Table 4.7

Mean Scores for Ethnic Groups in Pontiac
Regarding Basic Values*

	Mexican American Respondents	Puerto Rican American Respondents
1. All a person should want out of life in the way of a career is a secure, not too.....	5.57	5.62
2. When people are born, the success they are going to have is already in the cards....	2.30	1.97
3. The secret of happiness is not expecting too much out of life and being content...	2.62	2.95
4. Nothing is worth the sacrifice of moving away from one's parents.....	2.97	1.97
5. The best kind of job to have is one where you are part of an organization.....	3.72	4.75
6. Planning only makes a person unhappy since your plans hardly ever.....	3.52	2.55
7. Nowadays with world conditions the way they are, the wise person lives for today......	4.00	4.05

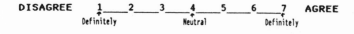

DISAGREE 1____2____3____4____5____6____7 AGREE
          Definitely   Neutral   Definitely

---

* Data analyzed by means of Kruskal-Wallis Chi Square. Connecting
  bars indicate statistical significance at one percent level of
  confidence.

Table 4.8

Mean Scores for Ethnic Groups in Pontiac
Regarding Education*

	Mexican American Respondents	Puerto Rican American Respondents
1. The future is bright for young people.	4.95	5.50
2. Education is more important today than past.	5.82	5.85
3. Education would be better if boys and girls separated.	2.95	2.65
4. Schools should not have dances.	2.85	2.97
5. Schools should have a racial mix of children.	6.30	6.50
6. Children should be taught more discipline in school.	6.42	6.50
7. Teachers are not as devoted to students as in past.	4.97	5.72
8. High school graduation isn't enough.	5.80	6.82
9. Students aren't as interested in learning as before in past.	5.17	5.67
10. Parents don't show enough interest in children's education.	5.05	4.15
11. Schools don't give enough say to parents.	4.15	4.72

DISAGREE 1____2____3____4____5____6____7 AGREE
          Definitely   Neutral   Definitely

* Data analyzed by means of Kruskal-Wallis Chi Square.
Connecting bars indicate statistical significance at one
percent level of confidence.

Table 4.9

Mean Scores for Ethnic Groups in Pontiac
Regarding School Subjects*

	Mexican American Respondents	Puerto Rican American Respondents
1. English language arts	6.90	6.88
2. Language arts for own language	6.70	6.55
3. Language arts for another language	5.53	5.25
4. Mathematics	6.98	6.98
5. Science	6.78	6.68
6. Computers	6.90	6.85
7. American history	6.50	6.63
8. History of own group	6.40	6.80
9. History of other groups	5.92	6.18
10. Music	5.48	5.73
11. Physical education	6.53	6.38
12. Hygiene and health	6.83	6.95
13. Sex education	5.82	5.45
14. Practical/technical training	6.70	6.78

UNIMPORTANT 1____2____3____4____5____6____7 IMPORTANT
             Definitely   Neutral   Definitely

---

* Data analyzed by means of Kruskal-Wallis Chi Square. Connecting bars indicate statistical significance at one percent level of confidence.

106

Table 4.10

Mean Scores for Ethnic Groups in Pontiac
Regarding the Desirability and Likelihood of Employment Prospects[*]

	How happy would you be if your son/ daughter became.....		What are the chances of your son/daughter becoming.....	
	Mexican American Respondents	Puerto Rican American Respondents	Mexican American Respondents	Puerto Rican American Respondents
1. a lawyer, a doctor, a director of a large company, etc. (a major professional position)?	6.95	6.67	5.27	5.87
2. an owner of a small business, small restaurant, a bookkeeper, (a minor professional position)?	6.57	6.12	5.45	5.52
3. a machinist, roofer, plumber, nurse, secretary (a skilled worker position)?	6.57	5.87	5.62	5.65
4. a road repair man, gas station attendant, a file clerk (a semiskilled worker position)?	5.42	4.25	4.97	3.82
5. a daily laborer in a factory or on a construction project, a house cleaner (an unskilled worker position)?	4.07	2.42	4.22	2.35

UNHAPPY 1___2___3___4___5___6___7 HAPPY
Definitely   Neutral   Definitely

CHANCES
POOR   1___2___3___4___5___6___7 CHANCES GOOD
Definitely   Neutral   Definitely

* Data analyzed by means of Kruskal-Wallis Chi Square. Connecting bars indicate statistical significance at one percent level of confidence.

5

The Perspectives of Mainstream
White Americans

In this chapter and the next, we switch our focus from
ethnic immigrant minorities in the United States to the
major, long established American "host" groups, starting
with white mainstreamers in this chapter and with black
mainstreamers in the next. These "host" groups are much
more than passive observers of the newcomers attempting to
survive and adjust in the New World. They are critical
players in the adjustment process itself. What do
mainstream Americans expect of immigrant newcomers? Are
newcomers seen as foreign intruders who have the potential
to disrupt established ways of life in American
communities? Are they potential changers of the
hierarchies of goals for which people strive? Or do they
threaten to change the established means of attaining goals
as has been found in earlier studies of ethnic immigrants
(Jones and Lambert, 1959; 1965; 1967)? In other words,
are immigrants a threat to the ongoing social system, or
are they potential sources of enrichment and strength for
that system? And since America is a nation of immigrants,
do the more established host groups have compassion for
newcomers and the problems of adjustment they face? These
are the questions we had in mind as we surveyed samples of
white and black Americans who share a common living space
with ethnic immigrants in urban centers in America.

WHITE MIDDLE-CLASS AMERICAN PERSPECTIVES

Heritage Culture Maintenance versus Assimilation

Consider first the perspectives of middle-class whites when asked whether cultural or racial minority groups in America should give up or maintain their traditional ways of life. The stand taken by our white middle-class group lies slightly above the neutral point on our scale (see Figure 5.1). Although less extreme than the responses of ethnic immigrant groups, these middle-class white parents, as a group, nonetheless express a discernible degree of appreciation for the American ideal of openness to newcomers and respect for heritage cultures. The stance they take on this basic issue also suggests that the more advantaged white Americans may empathize and understand the plight of immigrant families.

The arguments they use to support their overall position do project a sympathetic outlook (see Table 5.1). Judging from their responses, culture maintenance would mean allowing newcomers to express an important aspect of their identity, and for the nation as a whole it would mean keeping the best that different cultural groups have to offer. On the other hand, they recognize that heritage culture maintenance would also mean a diversification of cultural standards throughout the nation.

Sympathy for the plight of the newcomer is just as clearly expressed in their reactions to the standard arguments used in support of assimilation. They feel that if ethnic groups give up their traditional ways it would mean a loss for the nation in terms of ethnic group offerings and a loss of personal identity for those involved. They disagree with the idea that assimilation would make America more unified and cohesive, or that assimilation would contribute to a common cultural standard throughout the nation. What we find, in sum, is a fairly charitable attitude towards immigrant groups and a recognition that the nation has much to gain if heritage cultures are kept alive.

Heritage Culture and Language: How Much is Desirable?

When asked about how cultures can and should be kept alive (Table 5.2), our middle-class white parents are of the opinion that ethnic groups should keep their own styles of food, dress, music, and cultural values (such as how

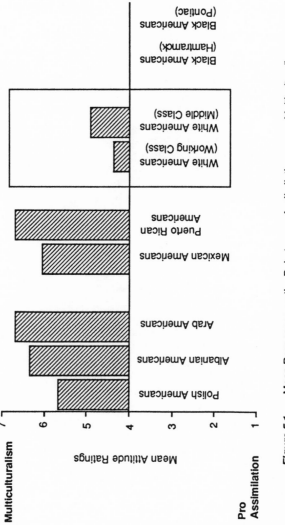

Figure 5.1   Mean Responses on the Debate over Assimilation versus Multiculturalism

children should be raised). They also agree that cultural history courses should be provided, preferably in church- or community-run classes. They do not, however, view public schools as the appropriate place for ethnic cultural courses nor do they endorse the idea of equal time in school for other cultural histories as for American history. But even in these cases, they are more neutral than expressly negative.

When asked whether ethnic groups of newcomers should keep their <u>languages</u> alive, they again are generally supportive up to the point of using ethnic languages for instruction in public schools (see Table 5.3). In their thinking, newcomers should use their languages for festivities, for religious services, as well as for interactions within the home and for instruction in community-run classes. They do not support ethnic language use in schools either on a part-time or on an equal time with English basis. Thus, their generous support for cultural history and heritage language usage stops at the public school doorstep.

The major point, however, is that they show consistent support for the maintenance of heritage languages if kept in the home and community but outside public schools. The signal we pick up here is that <u>private</u> (within the home and the ethnic community) expression of one's ethnicity is both acceptable and valuable, but the line is drawn sharply when ethnic expression becomes <u>public</u>. The host group's sensitivity to this apparently critical borderline deserves careful further study. It suggests to us that a compromise is expected from ethnic newcomers: keep your culture alive, but do so within ethnic boundaries; our system has many ethnic heritages to consider and public institutions, like the school system, are "common grounds" where a common language and a common way of life become preeminent.

The choice : Bilingualism or not for one's own children. Our white American parents were asked a different set of questions about their desires for their children's linguistic education, namely whether they wanted their own children to master a second language such as Spanish, French, or German (see Table 5.4). It is evident that these parents give bilingualism very strong support. They would definitely prefer their children to be bilingual in English and some world language (e.g., Spanish or French) rather than be limited to English only. In their minds,

inds, bilingual children would be more accepted in America, would have a greater sense of personal pride, would make their parents especially happy, would be helped in school work, would be more open and accepting of other ethnic and racial groups, and would be at an advantage in the world of work. Thus, the very strong endorsement of bilingualism given for their own children, when no specific second language is emphasized, reveals advantages that range from personal, to social, to occupational. It is likely that this recognition of bilingualism as a relatively precious attribute for their own children contributes to the appreciation these parents expressed for cultural diversity in the nation as a whole.

White Middle-Class Attitudes Towards Own and Other Groups

Attitudes. The white middle-class American parents not only hold strong and positive self-images (see Table 5.5), but they also have fairly favorable views of Puerto Rican Americans, black Americans, and Mexican Americans, all of whom they see as being hardworking, intelligent, smart with practical things, trustworthy, likable, and determined to succeed. At the same time, they recognize that these ethnic groups are not nearly as powerful as established white Americans are. Their overall favorableness towards other groups, however, is not indiscriminate; for example, they indicate that black Americans are particularly aggressive and violence prone. Nonetheless, compared to all other ethnic groups in Pontiac, the white middle-class parents have the most favorable attitudes towards all of the other ethnic groups in the community.

Social Distance. This generalized positive attitude toward other ethnic groups is reflected as well in the white middle-class group's willingness to accept members of other groups in various spheres of interpersonal relations (see Table 5.6). Thus, they find black, Mexican, and Puerto Rican Americans not only acceptable as co-citizens, but also as co-workers or partners in business, close neighbors, and close personal friends. Furthermore, they are the one ethnic group in the community most willing to accept members of other ethnic groups as family members through marriage (the means range from 3.80 to 4.85), the only exception being a qualified, neutral reaction to having   blacks as family members through marriage.   The main outcome, however,   deserves emphasis: the white middle-class American parents, those with the   most power and status by far, express the most open and accepting attitude   towards other ethnic and racial groups in their community.   We suspect there is more to this favorable disposition than a simple case of power security or of not being threatened economically by any of the other ethnic groups in the   community.   An alternative interpretation is that because they do have a   favorable and accurate self view, these more advantaged mainstream Americans can open their minds to ethnic minorities and view them with compassion and   appreciation.   They too are best placed to perpetuate the American ideal of accepting newcomers to the system and letting them be themselves.

THE PERSPECTIVES OF WHITE WORKING-CLASS AMERICANS

Of course, these favorable attitudes of the middle-class white Americans   do stem in part from their social and economic security vis-a-vis minority   ethnic groups in America.   Whites from working-class backgrounds on the other   hand have no such security.   It could well be that they would view ethnic   newcomers as potential threats who could, once they had facility with   English, not only compete, but even surpass them in the worlds of education   and work.   The motivational zeal of newcomers could be a particular threat.   Thus, we sensed from the start that we were working with two distinct groups   of white Americans who differed in terms of social class status and all that   that implies.

As we describe what was actually found in the analyses, the reader is   reminded of the special features of our working-class white American   subgroup: the large majority have a southern background; they have their own distinctive styles of speech, dress, and music that earns them the name of "hillbillies"; they come from low-income, low-education backgrounds; they are   long-term residents in America; and they are white.

Heritage Culture Maintenance Versus Assimilation

When asked whether cultural and racial minority groups living in America   should give up or maintain their traditional ways of life, our sample of working-class white parents take an essentially neutral stance, their mean score being 4.38 (see Figure 5.1). Although neutral, they still rank as the least enthusiastic of all groups surveyed in Pontiac or Hamtramck about multiculturalism. Nonetheless, they clearly do not endorse the assimilation alternative.

They are neutral as well in their reactions to the arguments commonly used to support culture maintenance (see Table 5.1), that is, they are neutral on the idea that, through multiculturalism, all groups could express an important part of their identity, that the nation would thereby keep the best that different groups have to offer, and that all people would then feel secure in their own-group identity. At the same time, they are also neutral about the idea that culture maintenance would divide America into segregated subunits.

They are not neutral, however, when asked about the consequences of ethnic groups giving up their traditional ways. When our basic question is worded in this way, the working-class whites believe that America would then have a more unified and cohesive makeup, that a common cultural standard would prevail across the nation, and that there would be a common base for intergroup understanding. Consistently, they tend to reject the idea that assimilation would force ethnic groups to give up something valuable or that the nation would lose the best that different cultural and racial groups have to offer. In sum, although they do not take a hostile, negative position against culture maintenance, the working-class white parents instead are neutral on the general debate question and only through their stronger endorsements of assimilationist views over culture maintenance arguments do they show a bias toward assimilation and hence some doubts about multiculturalism.

Heritage Culture and Language: How Much is Desirable? The working class white parents are consistent in the reactions they give to questions about how far ethnic groups should go in trying to maintain their cultures (see Table 5.2). They show low-level support for keeping heritage cultural styles of food, dress, and music, and for maintaining cultural values, such as distinctive modes of child rearing. And it would be all right (no more, no less) to have culture history courses taught in church-run or community-run classes. However, a sharp line is drawn at

the level of public school involvement: education about
cultures on a part-time or equal-time basis is   definitely
rejected as a proposal.

The working-class white parents express a basically
similar view about ethnic <u>language</u> maintenance (see Table
5.3).   They are not even certain   if   any language other
than English should ever be used in America, and they
question whether heritage languages should be used for
ethnic festivities, or   within the family.   Learning to
read   and write through church-run or   community-run
classes is acceptable, but public schools should not be
involved either on a part-time or equal-time basis.

<u>Bilingualism or not?   The choice for one's own children</u>.
Even though the working-class white parents have doubts
about immigrant newcomers to America   keeping their
heritage languages alive while learning English, they
nonetheless clearly favor bilingualism over monolingualism
for their own   offspring (see Table 5.4).   The advantages
they see for this form of   bilingualism are that it would
help their children get good marks in school,   it would
make it evident that they were intelligent,   and it would
enhance   the children's chances of obtaining certain jobs
that monolinguals could not likely get.   Being bilingual
would also bring status and respect to their   own group, it
would help their children to be open and relaxed with
others in the neighborhood, and permit them to feel a sense
of pride about who they   are.   It is noteworthy that for
all groups surveyed, including working-class white parents,
the bilingual alternative for one's own children is
significantly more attractive than the monolingual option.

Endorsing bilingualism for their own children while
discouraging or playing down the development of bilingual
skills for ethnic group children represents an interesting
double standard.   It suggests that these parents have their
suspicions about multiculturalism and that ethnic
minorities who perpetuate their languages pose a particular
threat to national unity.   At   the same time, it is
perfectly all right and even important for established
Americans to become bilingual.

**Working-Class Americans' Attitudes Toward Own and
Other Ethnic Groups**

<u>Attitudes</u>.   Our sample of working class white parents have

very positive   images about their own group (Table 5.5)
whom they see as being especially   likable, powerful,
intelligent, law-abiding, nonviolent, trustworthy, smart
with practical things, and determined to succeed.   They do
not view themselves as being aggressive or violent.   This
very favorable own-group perspective, however,   does not
generalize to any other ethnic group in the   community.
They do not see Puerto Rican, Mexican, or black Americans
as   being similar to them in any way (means range between
1.68 and 1.80), in   fact, they view each of these other
groups as lazy, un-American, unintelligent, untrustworthy,
unlikable, and not determined to succeed.   In   short, our
working-class whites show no affection for any ethnic or
racial group other than their own.   This highly
group-centered view contrasts   sharply with that of
middle-class whites who, as described earlier, have a more
balanced outlook on their own and other ethnic groups and
who are not   nearly as "prowhite" nor as "antiethnic" as
are their working-class counterparts.

Social Distance.   The social distance ratings convey the
same message,   (see Table 5.6).   In fact the most positive
thing one can say about the working-class white group's
willingness to accept others is that having   Mexican,
Puerto Rican, or black Americans as co-workers is what
offends them   the least, but even then their ratings (which
range between 3.08 and 3.38)   are far from positive.   On
the issue of accepting other ethnic groups as co-citizens,
the working-class white parents seem very protective and
exclusive,   indicating that they are not even willing to
accept black Americans as American citizens.   Furthermore,
they clearly do not want black, Puerto Rican, or Mexican
Americans as close personal friends or as neighbors and
they particularly draw a sharp line at accepting members of
these groups into their families through marriage (means
range between 1.30 and 1.43, meaning essentially "not at
all willing").   The line drawn is straight and clear:
White Americans are the only ones who are acceptable as
family members through marriage, as friends, neighbors,
co-workers, and as American citizens   (means in this case
range between 6.48 and 6.80).

Value Orientations and Parental Expectations for their Children: Cross Group Comparisons

Here we broaden our base of comparison to include both working and middle-class White groups and the two Hispanic groups, with the aim of seeing how compatible the value systems are of these four groups who share a common living space in Pontiac. The questions we have in mind are: Since children's education takes place in fully integrated, common public schools, are the more established mainstream American parents at odds with ethnic minority parents in terms of their values, their attitudes toward public schooling and the expectations they have for their children? Or might there be a basic overlap or similarity of values, attitudes and expectations among these various ethnic groups, a type of "common" value system?

Value Orientations

The results for the Kluckhohn scale of values are presented in Table 5.7, and what emerges are interesting contrasts among groups on the value dimensions of activism versus passivism, individualism versus collectivism and "future" orientation versus "present" orientation. The sharpest contrast is that between the middle-class and working-class white groups, with the middle-class groups generally the most activistic-individualistic-future oriented and the working-class groups the least, even less so than the Mexican and Puerto Rican American groups. Thus, the middle-class white parents reject, more than any other group, (a) an emphasis on security in career choice, (b) a belief in fate, (c) a tendency to be content with what one has, (d) the idea of losing oneself in a secure organization, (e) the belief that planning makes one unhappy, and (f) the philosophy of living for today. In contrast, the working-class white group, even though their profile is in a similar direction, are much closer to the neutral position on several of these value dimensions. Of all Pontiac groups surveyed, they are closest to the neutral position on the fate issue, on being content with one's lot, on the futility of making plans, and, along with the Puerto Rican group, more prone to seek work that makes them part of an organization. Not only is the contrast in values most pronounced between middle and working-class white groups, but in addition, the working-class whites express values, in several instances, more like that of Puerto Rican and Mexican Americans--the groups they keep at extreme social distances--than like the middle-class whites.   Thus, to the   extent that middle-class whites represent the ideal American value profile (strongly activistic, individualistic, future oriented, and thus achievement motivated), we find that the working-class white parents are consistently less committed to that ideal, even less so than the two major Hispanic groups who live in the same community.

Attitudes Towards Public Education

Both middle and working-class white parents agree on the importance of education: education, they contend, is more important now than in the past, and a high school graduation is no guarantee of employment nowadays (Table 5.8).   This strong sentiment, in fact, is shared by all groups interviewed and one is forced to question what parents signify by this cross-group consensus.   Since all but one of our groups are from lower, working class socioeconomic backgrounds, the belief that high school graduation is insufficient to get a good job is worrisome because most children from these backgrounds have great difficulty graduating from high school.   Thus, a widely transmitted myth that a high school degree isn't worth much could have a powerful dampening effect on students' motivation to persevere in school.   On the other hand, for the middle-class white group, the propagation of the same belief could act as a positive motivator for their children to get through high school and go on from there.

With regard to the structure of public schools, our two groups of white parents clash in their views of certain basic features of American public education.   Both groups, along with the two Hispanic groups, reject the idea of separating boys and girls and all groups show support for coed activities such as dances and the like. However, when asked if schools should have a mix of ethnically and racially different children, the middle-class white parents, along with the two Hispanic groups, strongly endorse the idea of integrated schools while the working-class white group essentially rejects the idea (see Table 5.8).   This striking contrast very likely reflects the regional origins of our working-class white sample;

their thinking reminds one of an old-fashioned, deep-South segregationist point of view. Even so, it is a socially dysfunctional attitude, and one can easily imagine the conflicts these parents and their children must have in a very ethnically mixed city like Pontiac with a fully integrated urban school system.

The Roles of Teachers, Students, and Parents in Public Education. There are no comparable discordant points of view when the two white groups were asked the standard questions about public education. Both agree that children should be taught more discipline in school, and that teachers could show somewhat more devotion. The two white groups are neutral in their reactions to the statement that students nowadays are less interested in learning, and that schools don't give parents enough say. They differ however in their reactions to the idea that parents don't show interest in their children's education: the working-class whites tend to disagree while the middle-class whites agree.

The Relative Importance of Various Curriculum Subject Matter. Similarly, there is a good deal of between-group agreement on the relative importance of various school subjects. Nearly all the school subjects listed (see Table 5.9) are seen as important, from math, science, computers, history, and music, to physical education, and technical/practical training. The working-class whites, however, are essentially neutral on the importance of English language arts, or history other than American history. In fact, they feel minority cultural histories are not important, nor is sex education. These perspectives of the working-class white parents also bring them into disagreement not only with middle-class whites, but with the two Hispanic groups as well.

Education and the World of Work. When asked how they would feel if their children were to end up in various types of careers, both groups, as expected, would be most content if their children reached professional career levels and least content if they only reached unskilled or semiskilled levels (see Table 5.10). More revealing are the group differences on the likelihood that their children will actually achieve high status career positions, since the odds of completing education and becoming prepared for high status jobs are very different for the two white groups.

While the middle-class white parents realize the chances
are very good that their children will reach high status
positions, the working-class white parents believe that
their children are likely to end up in unskilled worker
positions, unpleasant as that prospect is. In fact, the
working-class white group has the lowest occupational
expectations for their children of all groups in the
community, much lower than those of the Puerto Rican
Americans or middle-class whites, and lower even than the
Mexican Americans who, although not overly optimistic, at
least expect their children to compete for skilled worker
positions.

IN PERSPECTIVE

What answers can we now provide for the research
questions we asked ourselves about mainstream white
Americans?   How do our samples of whites feel about
multiculturalism and assimilation and do their perspectives
on these issues clash with those of ethnic newcomers?

The research outcomes force us to give two quite
different answers, one for those whites with middle-class
socioeconomic backgrounds and a second for whites with
working class backgrounds. Our middle-class white parents
revealed a surprisingly favorable perspective on the issues
dealing with multiculturalism, one that suggests a basic
understanding and appreciation of the adjustment pressures
faced by ethnic newcomers. This we infer from the
favorable attitudes expressed towards each of the ethnic
groups in the community, in the very positive personal
attributions they assign each group, and in their
willingness to interact with other groups at all levels of
social distance. The generosity extended to the issue of
heritage culture and language maintenance for all
ethnolinguistic groups, and the idea of keeping heritage
cultures and languages alive in the home and the ethnic
community. The line of tolerance was drawn at the idea of
involving public schools. Instruction via languages other
than English was considered inappropriate, even though
such instruction was encouraged if kept in community-run
classes. For their own children, however, bilingualism,
developed through schooling, was highly prized for its
social, intellectual, and career related consequences. We
interpret this comparatively strong support of
multiculturalism and the appreciation of ethnic newcomers

as a derivative of the strong and favorable self-view our white middle-class parents displayed, a view that recognized their social position as being advantaged and backed by social power. The generally favorable and secure attitude towards own group appears to generalize to blacks as well as ethnic immigrant newcomers.

At the same time as we discovered strong, supportive allies of multiculturalism among the white middle-class parents, we also uncovered a much more distant, unfriendly and unappreciative attitude towards multiculturalism and ethnic newcomers among our sample of white working-class parents. Because this group comprises mainly people who have come to Detroit from various south and deep-south states, we realize that we can in no sense generalize these results to other working-class white Americans. Nonetheless, this particular working-class group, perhaps because they have their own distinctive American cultural heritage, takes a neutral, not a negative, stand on the debate about multiculturalism versus cultural assimilation. But their attitudes towards any other ethnic group in the community are negative to the point of disdainful. They assign no favorable attributes to any group other than white Americans, and they keep all nonwhite American groups at extreme social distances, ethnic newcomers as well as blacks. This negative attitude surfaced in their responses to questions about ethnic newcomers keeping heritage cultures and languages alive. They were also strongly against culture and language training, other than "American", in the public schools. They saw substantial advantages, however, for their own children if they were to become bilingual, and the double standard implied appeared to pass without notice.

The values of the working-class white group, measured on the Kluckhohn scale, were also discordant, making that group's profile of values more at odds with middle-class whites than were the profiles of the two Hispanic groups. Similarly, their stand against racially and ethnically mixed public schooling not only made them the distinctively odd group in the community, but also the only group that appeared racist in outlook, as though they were personally threatened by ethnic groups of all sorts.

In sum, then, what we have discovered here are symptoms of a community in which the more established, mainstream whites separated themselves into two groups, one that appears to be an appreciative ally of multiculturalism in America (the case of the white middle-class parental group), and a second that appears to be a suspicious, unfriendly, and potentially threatened enemy of cultural and racial diversity (the case of the white working-class group).   This sharp diversity of perspectives among white Americans, who may appear to be a homogeneous group, very likely complicates the task that ethnic newcomers and long-term minorities face in adjusting to life in urban America.   But to complete our description of intergroup relations in this urban center, we have another critically important community group--black Americans--to bring into the total picture.   This we do in the next chapter.

Table 5.1

Responses of White American Respondents
Regarding Assimilation and Culture Maintenance*

Culture Maintenance Arguments:

	White Working Class Respondents	White Middle Class Respondents
Arguments Against		
All people living in America will not have a common base for understanding each other	3.21	3.60
There will be different languages and cultural standards throughout America	3.74	4.95
America will be divided into segregated units	4.00	3.90
Arguments For		
People will be allowed to express an important part of their identity	4.31	5.52
People will feel secure in their group identity, and this will make them open and sympathetic to other groups	4.18	4.65
The nation can keep the best that different cultural and racial groups have to offer	4.21	5.30

Assimilation Arguments:

	White Working Class Respondents	White Middle Class Respondents
Arguments For		
All people living in America will have a common base for understanding each other	4.90	3.32
The same language and cultural standards will exist for all Americans	5.08	3.52
America will be unified and cohesive	5.00	2.95
Arguments Against		
People will be robbed of a very important part of their personal identity	3.74	5.45
People will have been forced to give up something valuable, and this will make them hostile toward others	3.38	4.85
The nation loses the best that different cultural and racial groups have to offer	3.08	5.47

DISAGREE 1 Definitely 2 3 4 Neutral 5 6 7 Definitely AGREE

* Data analyzed by means of Kruskal-Wallis Chi Square. Connecting bars indicate statistical significance at one percent level of confidence.

Table 5.2

Mean Scores for White Respondents
Regarding Retention of the Heritage Culture*

In your opinion, how far should ethnic group go in maintaining their cultures and traditions?	White Working Class Respondents	White Middle Class Respondents
1. Step A: Since their cultures and traditions are not American, they should not be maintained.	4.78	2.40
2. Step B: Keep their own cultural styles of foods, dress, songs and dances.	4.59	5.47
3. Step C: Keep their own cultural values, such as how children should behave with parents, husbands with wives, dating practices, etc.	4.19	5.05
4. Step D: Attend courses about their own cultural history and traditions, not in public schools but in church-run or community-run classes.	4.70	4.87
5. Step E: Have courses about their own cultural history and traditions taught in public schools.	2.16	3.77
6. Step F: Have equal time in schools spent on their cultural history and traditions as on American history & traditions.	2.27	3.67

DISAGREE   1____2____3____4____5____6____7   AGREE
            Definitely   Neutral   Definitely

---

* Data analyzed by means of Kruskal-Wallis Chi Square. Connecting bars indicate statistical significance at one percent level of confidence.

124

Table 5.3

Mean Scores for White Respondents
Regarding the Maintenance of the Heritage Language*

In your opinion, how far should ethnic groups go in using their own languages?	White Working Class Respondents	White Middle Class Respondents
1. Step A: Cultural groups whose language is not Standard English should never use their own language.	3.92	2.25
2. Step B: Use their own language for festival days, cultural songs, traditional stories, prayers and religious services.	3.97	5.55
3. Step C: Use their own language for speaking with older family members, like grandparents.	3.45	5.57
4. Step D: Use their own language for most or all speaking within the family.	3.92	4.22
5. Step E: Learn to read and write their own language not through school, but through church-run or community-run classes.	5.45	4.87
6. Step F: Use their language for part of the teaching and learning in public schools.	2.42	3.22
7. Step G: Give equal time in schools to the use of their language as to Standard English.	2.39	2.87

DISAGREE 1____2____3____4____5____6____7 AGREE
          Definitely   Neutral   Definitely

---

* Data analyzed by means of Kruskal-Wallis Chi Square.
  Connecting bars indicate statistical significance at one percent
  level of confidence.

Table 5.4

Mean Scores Regarding the Consequences of Bilingualism*

Would they:	White Working Class Respondents			White Middle Class Respondents		
	If your son/daughter were bilingual	If your son/daughter spoke only a foreign language	If your son/daughter spoke only English	If your son/daughter were bilingual	If your son/daughter spoke only a foreign language	If your son/daughter spoke only English
1. feel accepted in America?	6.38	2.80	4.73	6.65	4.18	6.48
2. feel a sense of pride?	6.13	3.05	4.28	6.28	4.20	6.00
3. make their parents happy?	6.43	2.53	4.05	6.15	3.88	5.55
4. feel open and relaxed with others?	6.08	3.15	4.64	6.08	3.40	6.00
5. bring status and respect to their group?	5.85	2.90	4.28	5.80	3.58	5.59
6. stand out as different?	4.82	5.05	4.10	3.18	5.28	2.21
7. be treated like second-class citizens?	2.49	4.95	3.51	1.78	4.20	1.90
8. get good marks in school?	5.30	2.53	3.78	5.63	2.40	5.03
9. have a chance for certain jobs others can't get?	5.77	2.21	3.54	6.23	3.23	4.41
10. be sympathetic to people from different groups?	4.28	3.05	3.08	5.08	4.83	4.55
11. show intelligence?	5.36	2.82	3.95	5.23	3.40	4.03

NO 1̲_____2̲_____3̲_____4̲_____5̲_____6̲_____7̲ YES
    Definitely   Neutral   Definitely

---

* Data analyzed by means of Wilcoxon sign-ranks test. Connecting bars indicate statistical significance at one percent level of confidence.

Table 5.5

Mean Attribution Ratings of Own Group and Other Groups*

How ..... are	White Working Class Respondents				White Middle Class Respondents			
	most Puerto Rican Americans	most Mexican Americans	most Black Americans	most White Americans	most Puerto Rican Americans	most Mexican Americans	most Black Americans	most White Americans
1. hardworking	2.80	2.43	2.60	5.93	5.35	5.45	5.26	5.56
2. aggressive or violent	3.68	3.60	4.03	3.20	3.81	3.69	4.21	3.66
3. American	3.10	2.95	3.10	6.00	5.08	5.20	5.45	5.98
4. likely to stick together as a group	4.53	4.60	5.05	5.80	5.90	5.70	5.63	5.08
5. powerful	3.18	3.23	3.80	6.18	2.70	2.95	4.93	6.13
6. similar to me	1.68	1.70	1.80	6.33	3.92	4.10	4.33	5.77
7. intelligent at school	2.95	2.88	2.80	6.15	4.92	5.22	5.21	5.79
8. smart with practical things	3.08	2.98	3.00	6.10	4.79	5.03	5.15	5.55
9. trustworthy	2.58	2.55	2.48	6.10	5.22	5.28	5.28	5.60
10. law-abiding (good citizen)	2.78	2.58	2.88	6.10	5.32	5.49	5.36	5.69
11. unfairly treated	2.55	2.53	2.80	5.00	4.82	4.70	4.48	3.15
12. likable	3.20	3.20	2.98	6.30	5.63	5.73	5.65	5.98
13. determined to succeed	2.98	3.03	2.98	6.63	4.97	5.18	5.10	5.63

NOT AT ALL 1 Definitely 2 3 4 Neutral 5 6 7 VERY Definitely

* Data analyzed by means of Wilcoxon sign-ranks test. Connecting bars indicate statistical significance at one percent level of confidence.

127

Table 5.6

Mean Social Distance Ratings*

How willing are you personally to accept these people?	White Working Class Respondents				White Middle Class Respondents			
	most Puerto Rican Americans	most Mexican Americans	most Black Americans	most White Americans	most Puerto Rican Americans	most Mexican Americans	most Black Americans	most White Americans
1. As a family member through marriage?	1.43	1.33	1.30	6.80	4.88	4.85	3.80	6.50
2. As a close personal friend?	2.50	2.28	2.25	6.48	5.95	6.03	5.90	6.25
3. As a close neighbor in my neighborhood or apartment building?	3.00	2.80	2.50	6.60	5.80	5.98	5.68	6.45
4. As a co-worker or partner at work?	3.38	3.28	3.08	6.63	6.28	6.30	6.20	6.53
5. As a citizen of the U.S.A.?	2.88	2.85	2.95	6.68	6.48	6.55	6.50	6.70

NOT AT ALL   1   2   3   4   5   6   7   VERY

Definitely   Neutral   Definitely

* Data analyzed by means of Wilcoxon sign-ranks test. Connecting bars indicate statistical significance at one percent level of confidence.

128

Table 5.7

Mean Scores for White Respondents
Regarding Basic Values*

	White Working Class Respondents	White Middle Class Respondents
1. All a person should want out of life in the way of a career is a secure, not too.....	4.02	3.20
2. When people are born, the success they are going to have is already in the cards....	3.45	1.82
3. The secret of happiness is not expecting too much out of life and being content...	3.70	2.07
4. Nothing is worth the sacrifice of moving away from one's parents.....	2.05	2.05
5. The best kind of job to have is one where you are part of an organization.....	4.45	3.27
6. Planning only makes a person unhappy since your plans hardly ever.....	3.77	2.05
7. Nowadays with world conditions the way they are, the wise person lives for today......	3.72	2.62

DISAGREE 1____2____3____4____5____6____7 AGREE
         Definitely   Neutral   Definitely

---

* Data analyzed by means of Kruskal-Wallis Chi Square. Connecting bars indicate statistical significance at one percent level of confidence.

129

Table 5.8

Mean Scores for White Respondents
Regarding Education*

	White Working Class Respondents	White Middle Class Respondents
1. The future is bright for young people.	5.70	5.00
2. Education is more important today than past.	6.25	6.35
3. Education would be better if boys and girls separated.	2.55	2.10
4. Schools should not have dances.	1.90	2.05
5. Schools should have a racial mix of children.	3.37	5.97
6. Children should be taught more discipline in school.	5.12	5.92
7. Teachers are not as devoted to students as in past.	4.70	4.62
8. High school graduation isn't enough.	6.00	6.15
9. Students aren't as interested in learning as in past.	4.57	4.05
10. Parents don't show enough interest in children's education.	3.67	4.57
11. Schools don't give enough say to parents.	4.32	4.30

DISAGREE 1____2____3____4____5____6____7 AGREE
          Definitely   Neutral   Definitely

* Data analyzed by means of Kruskal-Wallis Chi Square.
  Connecting bars indicate statistical significance at one
  percent level of confidence.

Table 5.9

Mean Scores for White Respondents
Regarding School Subjects*

	White Working Class Respondents	White Middle Class Respondents
1. English language arts	4.30	6.95
2. Language arts for own language	Not Applicable	
3. Language arts for another language	4.13	5.35
4. Mathematics	6.18	6.83
5. Science	6.60	6.58
6. Computers	6.80	6.40
7. American history	5.35	6.43
8. History of own group	Not Applicable	
9. History of other groups	3.38	5.65
10. Music	5.38	5.80
11. Physical education	6.03	5.85
12. Hygiene and health	6.13	6.10
13. Sex education	3.28	5.85
14. Practical/technical training	5.98	6.25

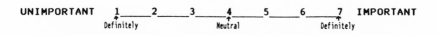

UNIMPORTANT 1____2____3____4____5____6____7 IMPORTANT
      Definitely   Neutral   Definitely

* Data analyzed by means of Kruskal-Wallis Chi Square. Connecting bars
  indicate statistical significance at one percent level of confidence.

131

Table 5.10

Mean Scores for White Respondents
Regarding the Desirability and Likelihood of Employment Prospects*

	How happy would you be if your son/daughter became.....		What are the chances of your son/daughter becoming.....	
	White Working Class Respondents	White Middle Class Respondents	White Working Class Respondents	White Middle Class Respondents
1. a lawyer, a doctor, a director of a large company, etc. (a <u>major professional</u> position)?	6.05	6.40	4.05	6.00
2. an owner of a small business, small restaurant, a bookkeeper, (a <u>minor professional</u> position)?	5.74	6.07	4.16	5.62
3. a machinist, roofer, plumber, nurse, secretary (a <u>skilled worker</u> position)?	4.66	5.95	4.34	4.92
4. a road repair man, gas station attendant, a file clerk (a <u>semiskilled worker</u> position)?	3.47	4.42	4.58	3.40
5. a daily laborer in a factory or on a construction project, a house cleaner (an <u>unskilled worker</u> position)?	2.32	3.42	4.71	2.85

UNHAPPY   1___2___3___4___5___6___7 HAPPY
          Definitely   Neutral   Definitely

CHANCES
POOR   1___2___3___4___5___6___7 CHANCES GOOD
          Definitely   Neutral   Definitely

---

* Data analyzed by means of Kruskal-Wallis Chi Square. Connecting bars indicate statistical significance at one percent level of confidence.

6

The Perspectives of Black Americans

In the long run, the views of black Americans on questions
of multiculturalism, assimilation, national unity, or
educational policy may be the most meaningful of all. In
the debate about assimilation versus culture maintenance,
attention is usually restricted to recently arrived
immigrant groups and their modes of adjusting or
accommodating to "mainstream American values". One
question we have is whether "mainstream" effectively means
white America or are blacks also implicated? Certainly
blacks contribute to and help define the American value
system, but they have been struggling so long and hard for
an equitable place within the American infrastructure that
they are usually thought of more as a "special problem" to
America than as equals in the development of national
values. Consequently, when societal issues like
multiculturalism and assimilation are debated at the
pedagogical, political, or scientific levels, the views of
blacks are often treated apart or not considered at all,
even though their contributions to the American position
on such issues are among the oldest and most stimulating of
all (see Lambert & Taylor, 1987).

How societal issues like multiculturalism, assimilation and educational policy are dealt with and resolved at the community level has a profound impact on blacks, and blacks' attitudes and reactions to community decisions on such issues ultimately determine how effective policy changes will be.   For instance, when school systems divert human and financial resources to bilingual/bicultural programs to enable new immigrant children to be fully educated, blacks might very reasonably see this focus on newcomers as slighting blacks and their special needs. And being slighted could lead to resentment which could ultimately skuttle any attempts at educational improvement. It is in this sense that we see black Americans' perspectives as pivotal (see Lambert & Taylor, 1983; 1987).

The black perspective is also rarely solicited in the context of debates about language, especially when the focus is on bilingualism or multilingualism. The reasoning seems to be that while blacks are clearly a disadvantaged minority group, language is not a serious problems for them.   Thus, blacks are left out of the equation.   The alternative of course is to regard any program or policy that is put into place for one group as having important implications for all other groups in the social system, especially a visible minority that uses a distinctive form of the national language.

It follows from the importance we ascribe to the views of black people in America that we would have given at least equal treatment to them in our greater Detroit surveys.   In fact, we gave double attention to blacks, drawing one sample of black parents from the public school rosters in Hamtramck and a second sample from the school rosters in Pontiac.   Although both black communities consisted of mainly poor, working class families, each was part of a quite distinctive ethnic mosaic, as the data so far presented have demonstrated. Our research questions at this point were: How do these black Americans view such common societal issues as multiculturalism, multilingualism, and educational reform? What role do they see for themselves in the development of policies on such issues?   Do their perspectives clash with those of ethnic newcomers or those of mainstream whites?

Heritage Culture Maintenance Versus Assimilation

When asked their opinions about whether cultural or racial minority groups should give up or maintain their distinctive traditional ways when they come to America, the black American parents favor the multiculturalism alternative although the extent of black endorsement is much stronger in Hamtramck than in Pontiac (see Figure 6.1).   Since the wording of this basic question required respondents to consider their own ethnic or racial group as well as other groups, the stand taken by blacks may reflect a personal involvement with black culture as well as an endorsement of the general principle of cultural and racial diversity in America.

The Hamtramck-Pontiac difference in degree of endorsement is of interest.   One possible interpretation is that the <u>average</u> level of support for culture maintenance is higher when all groups surveyed in one community are considered (the average for Hamtramck is 6.21) and compared with the average for the other community (5.34 for Pontiac). Thus, the black parents may be sensitive to community norms on this issue, and adjust their strength of endorsement accordingly.   Another possible interpretation of the difference in the stands of the two black groups is that the group average for the black parents in Pontiac is very similar in degree of endorsement to that of the more "powerful" middle-class white group in the same setting, which is less   extreme than that of the two Hispanic groups who have become ethnic rivals of blacks in that community. Thus in Pontiac, black parents may be made more aware of the "American" norm (or norms) on the issue because of the presence of two mainstream American white groups. In Hamtramck there is no equivalent American reference group.   In fact, the most established, long-term co-residents of blacks in Hamtramck are the Polish Americans, and they give a comparatively strong endorsement of culture maintenance. These and other possible interpretations simply highlight the need for f u r t h e r r e s e a r c h o n this i n t e r e s t i n g community-to-community difference in ethnic group perspectives.

In both settings, however, there is a consistency in reasoning behind the position taken on the multiculturalism issue, and the logical support is more pronounced in Hamtramck than in Pontiac (see Table 6.1). The black respondents argue that if ethnic or racial

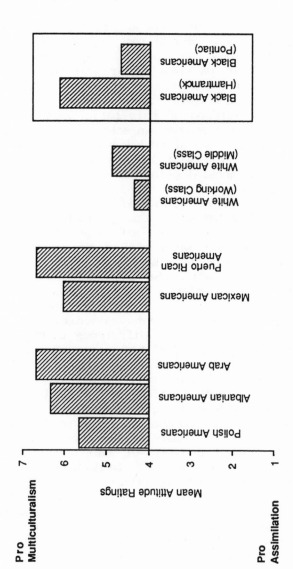

Figure 6.1 Mean Responses on the Debate over Assimilation versus Multiculturalism

groups were to give up their traditional ways, it would not necessarily foster a common base for understanding, or a common cultural and linguistic standard across America, nor would it necessarily help to create a more unified and cohesive nation.   Instead, they argue that giving up heritage cultures would mean that people would lose an important aspect of their identity, that it would generate hostility towards other groups, and that it would represent a national loss of the best that each group has to offer. Nonetheless, black parents register a realization that culture maintenance could involve a diversification of cultural and linguistic standards throughout the land which could contribute to social divisions and segregation. The reserve shown here is very similar in extent to that of the middle-class white group in Pontiac who nonetheless displayed generally open-minded and sympathetic attitudes toward the multiculturalism alternative.

Heritage Culture and Language: How Much is Desirable? The basic data for the black parents on the question of maintaining their own Afro-American culture and traditions are presented in Table 6.2.   First of all, there is a consistent position on both culture and language maintenance for the Hamtramck black sample as compared to the Pontiac black sample. Considering the <u>culture maintenance</u> issue first, our samples of black parents clearly reject the idea that minority cultures and traditions are not American and therefore should not be maintained. They argue that blacks in general should keep their own styles of food, dress, music; that ethnic values dealing with child rearing and family relationship should be maintained; that courses about the cultural history of blacks should be taught in both community-run as well as public schools and be treated as fully as standard American history.   By taking a relatively strong stand on having ethnic histories taught in public schools, the black American parents pull away from an otherwise close match with the Polish American parents in Hamtramck, bringing blacks closer on the issue to the Arab and Albanian Americans.   Likewise in the Pontiac setting, their stand on ethnic histories in public schools brings them more in line with Mexican and Puerto Rican American parents than either the white middle-class or the white working-class parents who have reservations about the involvement of public schools in culture maintenance.

On the issue of <u>language maintenance</u>, black parents

have a slightly different overall policy, but one that is equally consistent (see Table 6.3). In general, they reject the idea that their heritage dialect is "nonAmerican" and thus should never be used. On the contrary, they strongly endorse its use for festivities, cultural activities, and religious services, and not only for conversations with older generation members, but for most communication within the family. They are more hesitant about the use of their form of a heritage language for instruction in public schools on either a part-time or half-time basis. Their neutral position on this delicate issue is similar to that of the Polish parents in Hamtramck and less like the Arab and Albanian parents who, as we have seen, give a much stronger endorsement of heritage languages for part-time instruction in the public schools. In Pontiac, the neutrality of the black parents on the same issue makes them very similar to white middle-class parents and different from the Hispanic groups, especially the Puerto Rican parents who, as shown earlier, strongly favor the use of their heritage language in public school education.

The Choice: Bidialectism or Not for One's Own Children.
Black parents were asked to contemplate three alternatives for their own children: becoming fluent in both standard English and black English, fluent only in standard English and fluent only in black English. The question has special significance since English is the "native" language of black Americans, but it is not always the case that their children will become fluently bidialectal in both standard and black English. Nevertheless, the responses of our black American parents parallel closely those of ethnic immigrant groups who answered the same questions in terms of two distinct languages (Table 6.4). Thus, mastery of both dialects is rated as highly desirable; fluency in standard English only is slightly less desirable; and fluency in black English only is seen as a real handicap. A person limited to black English would not feel fully accepted in America; would not be open and relaxed when interacting with others; would stand out as different; would bring little status to his/her group; and most decidedly would not make his/her parents happy. On the practical side, a person with fluency only in black English would likely not obtain good grades in school or obtain a good job, nor would he/she be seen as intelligent. The standard English only alternative is regarded more

favorably, but the bidialectal alternative is more favorable still and its attractiveness is not only social and cultural in nature but practical and economic as well.

Black Parents Attitudes Towards Own and Other Ethnic Groups

Attitudes.   The attitudes of our two samples of black parents toward their own group and the other major ethnic groups in their respective communities are summarized in Table 6.5.   Both samples have very similar views of black Americans and in both instances the self-view is basically positive,   although not always flattering.   It is more restrained, not exaggerated as was the case for most other parental groups.   For instance, black parents describe themselves foremost as being very American and very unfairly treated; they also see themselves as likable, determined to succeed, smart with practical things, intelligent at school, and hardworking.   At the same time, they see themselves as fairly aggressive and violent and only so-so in terms of trustworthiness.

Their views of other ethnic groups are equally realistic and sobering.   Working-class blacks in America live with a good deal of violence and aggression in their communities.   In their responses, they involve themselves as instigators of this violence, but they also see all other ethnic groups as equally violent, and in certain cases, more so. White Americans, in fact, are seen as the most violent or aggressive group, while ethnic immigrant groups are relatively less so. Polish Americans in Hamtramck are rated as the least violent or aggressive, significantly less so than black Americans. On most other traits as well, black parents project a basically favorable, friendly attitude toward Polish Americans.

White Americans are seen as especially powerful as well as aggressive and violent, and strongly American. Our black parents draw interesting contrasts between themselves and whites: they see blacks as being just as American as whites, just as intelligent and smart, but much less powerful and very much more unfairly treated. These signs of resentment are evident as well in blacks' views of other ethnic groups, for no other group is seen as any more intelligent or smart than black Americans, none are as American (not even the Puerto Ricans), and although Mexican, Puerto Rican, and Vietnamese Americans are also seen as unfairly treated, none are as unfairly treated as blacks.

Not all other ethnic groups agree with the estimates of intergroup attitudes presented by our black samples. In Hamtramck, the Polish and black American groups show mutual respect and appreciation for one another. In Pontiac, the middle-class whites show the most favorable attitudes towards blacks, seeing them much as they see themselves--hardworking, American, intelligent, smart, and likable. They see blacks also as unfairly treated, a description they do not use for themselves. In fact, middle-class whites (Table 5.5) see blacks as more trustworthy and law-abiding (M = 5.28 and 5.36) than blacks see themselves (M = 4.13 and 4.26). On the other hand, Mexican American, and to a lesser extent Puerto Rican American parents (Table 4.5), see blacks as much less hardworking and much more aggressive than blacks see themselves. The working-class whites are the most anti-black by far. In fact, they reveal a crude racist attitude, rating blacks as essentially lazy, nonAmerican, unintelligent, untrustworthy, not unfairly treated, and not likable. Again, caution is needed: this very negative attitude may be a remnant of outdated, lower social class Southern stereotypes about blacks that our working class white sample of parents may have brought to Detroit with them from their home states.

Social Distance. Although the black parents prefer closer social relationships with other blacks, both in Hamtramck and Pontiac, they still are open and friendly to other groups as well (see Table 6.6). In Hamtramck, they show a preference for Polish over Arab or Albanian Americans as potential friends, neighbors, and co-workers, and in Pontiac, their gestures of goodwill include a willingness to accept white, Mexican, and Puerto Rican Americans as potential family members through marriage. As already noted, although these same groups have reservations about marriage contacts with blacks, they nonetheless are very willing to accept blacks as personal friends, neighbors, and co-workers. It is only the working-class whites who reject all types of black-white social contacts.

Overall, then, our two samples of black parents project a favorable perception of themselves as being hardworking, intelligent, and resourceful people who are solidly American. They are also aggressive and violent, but no more so than other peoples, and they are relatively unfairly treated by society.   They appear to be aware of which other groups appreciate them, for example, the Poles in Hamtramck and the middle-class whites in Pontiac, and they reciprocate favorable sentiments towards these potential friends.   They very likely realize that other groups have hostile and potentially racist views of blacks, for example the Arabs and Albanians in Hamtramck, and they rate these groups less favorably. However, they accept several other "non-American" ethnic newcomers (the Polish, Mexican and Puerto Rican Americans) as likable peoples who would be fully accepted by the blacks as neighbors, co-workers, friends, and even as family members through marriage.

Not only do blacks frequently refer to themselves as American, they also happen to be very similar on important social policy issues to mainstream middle-class white Americans who have the power and influence to shape policies in the Pontiac community.   In Hamtramck where there is no comparable mainstream white reference group, blacks' views on such issues are very similar to those of Polish Americans, the most established and most powerful ethnic group in that community. Of special interest to us is the possibility suggested by these findings that blacks may be as important contributors as whites to the "American culture" and to the "American value system", a possibility that is not commonly appreciated, if even recognized.

Parental Value Orientations and Expectations for Children: Cross Group Comparisons

Are there other clusters of attitudes on particular issues peculiar to our samples of black parents that help us to better understand their overall views about ethnic diversity and intergroup relations in the United States? Are their values and the expectations they have for their children out of line with those of other ethnic groups, and in particular with white Americans? These questions prompted us to make the following group comparisons.

Value Orientations

On the Kluckhohn value scales, the two samples of black parents have essentially a common profile of scores, except for a difference on the live-for-today item where the blacks in Hamtramck show slightly more agreement than the blacks in Pontiac (see Table 6.7). Otherwise, the value profile of both black American groups are very similar to those of middle-class white Americans in that they both shy away from a too secure life style, reject a fatalistic attitude toward life, reject being too easily content with one's lot in life, reject staying close to one's parents, avoid becoming too reliant on big organizations for occupations, support strongly the idea of planning for the future, and take an essentially neutral stand on living for today rather than worrying too much about tomorrow. This may be a good description of the American philosophy of life, or at least of the American approach to achievement (Rosen, 1959; McClelland, 1961), and it is interesting that both blacks and middle-class whites strongly endorse such a philosophy. No other ethnic group in Hamtramck is consistently in line with this set of values, not even the Polish Americans, and clearly not the Arab or Albanian Americans. In Pontiac, the Mexican, Puerto Rican, and working-class white parents each show deviations from the black and middle-class white groups on one dimension or another. Thus, these findings also lend support to the hypothesis that a distinctively American set of values or philosophy of life may be shaped not only by the high status, high power middle-class whites, but by blacks as well, indeed by blacks from very humble, working-class backgrounds.

Attitudes Toward Public Education

Black parents' opinions about public education and its effect on their children are in line with most other parental groups (see Table 6.8). Where such opinions are out of line, they are traceable to peculiar, non-American reactions from particular ethnic immigrant groups, not blacks. For instance, black American parents agree with other parental groups that the future looks fairly bright for their children, that education is more important today than in earlier times, that high school graduation does not guarantee a good job, that more discipline should be taught in schools, that teachers are not devoted enough to their work, and that students and parents are not interested enough in schooling. The points of disagreement are on the value the black parents attach to coeducational schools which does not jibe with the views of Arab and

Albanian parents, and on the value of <u>ethnically mixed</u> schools which does not jibe with our sample of working-class white parents.

When asked about the value of specific curriculum content for children in today's world, the black parents have the same scale of priorities that all other ethnic groups have, the only exception, again, being the white working-class group (see Table 6.9). All curriculum subjects listed were rated as important, with the highest ratings given to English language arts, math, science, computers, American history, own-group history, hygiene and health, and practical training. Thus, there is virtual consensus among all parental groups on what should be taught in school.

Education and the World of Work.   Black parents in both communities were asked our standard questions about a) how happy they would be if their children arrived at various levels of occupational achievement, and b) how likely it was that their children would ultimately attain positions at various occupational levels (see Table 6.10). The two black American samples have very similar expectations of how their children will fare; they differ only on the possibility that their children might not attain skilled working positions, and it is the blacks in Pontiac who would be more unhappy by such an outcome.

In general, black parents react very much like middle-class white parents in that both groups would, of course, be happy were their children to attain professional levels of occupation (the means are 6.50 and 6.40), and both would be somewhat unhappy if unskilled work was the best their children could look forward to achieving (3.35 and 3.42). This means that the black and middle-class white groups differ from working-class white and Puerto Rican American groups who would be more unhappy by an unskilled worker end point for their children. On the other hand, the Mexican American parents would be the least unhappy of all groups with unskilled work for their children.

When giving the odds for their children's ultimate success in the world of work, the black parents in Pontiac line up closely with the Mexican Americans and the working-class whites in the expectation that semiskilled and unskilled positions are a fairly strong likelihood, even though all three groups have hopes that their children will fare better. In contrast, Puerto Rican parents are very similar to middle-class whites since both groups say that it is unlikely that their children will fall below a skilled worker level. The same trend turns up in Hamtramck: black parents have expectations similar to Polish Americans who also seem more aware of current job realities than Albanian parents who reject the possibilities of unskilled work for their children. In summary, black American parents project a sense of hope for the occupational future of their children, along with a realistic awareness that finding work of any kind is difficult these days, and particularly so for young blacks.

IN PERSPECTIVE

By way of summary, what have we learned about black American perspectives on multiculturalism, multilingualism, and on public education's impact on the lives of their children? Are their perspectives consonant or dissonant with those of other ethnic minority groups in their communities or with mainstream white Americans? Since we surveyed separate samples of black parents in Hamtramck and Pontiac, we have a broad base for drawing several conclusions.

It becomes clear that black American parents are generally in favor of multiculturalism and against assimilation. The Hamtramck-Pontiac differences in degree of support for multiculturalism suggest to us that blacks are sensitive to and influenced by the dominant attitudes on this issue present in their respective communities. Thus in Hamtramck, black American parents have views that are very similar to those of the Polish Americans, while in Pontiac their views are particularly similar to those of the middle-class whites. In both sites, they give consistent arguments to bolster their stand (e.g., that pressures to assimilate would upset the real identities of ethnic minorities, and that the nation would lose the best that each ethnic group has to offer). At the same time, they recognize that multiculturalism would diversify the cultural norms of the nation, but this would not necessarily lead to disunity or social conflict. Thus, blacks strongly support the idea that ethnic groups should keep their cultural histories and traditions alive. This strong position favoring multiculturalism brings them especially close to the Arab and Albanian American parents

in Hamtramck and to the Mexican and Puerto Rican parents in
Pontiac. On the issue of introducing courses on heritage
cultures in the public schools, their supportive stand
draws them away from both middle-class and working-class
white groups.

On heritage language maintenance, black parents would
like their   children to develop mastery of both   black
English and standard American English. Having command of
black English only would, in their eyes, be dysfunctional
and inappropriate.   Their heritage dialect should be
fostered in the home and community, but they are   neutral
only to the idea that it be introduced into the curriculum
of the public schools. Thus, there is more black support
for introducing to the public education system their
heritage culture than for introducing their heritage
dialect. This position brings the black parental groups
more in line with Polish American parents in Hamtramck and
away from Arab and Albanian groups.   However, in Pontiac,
these views make black parents very similar to middle-class
whites and different from the two Hispanic parental groups.

The attitudes of black parents towards their own and
other ethnic groups are particularly instructive. Their
self-view is neither positive nor negative and thus,
relative to the other groups surveyed, it appears more
honest and realistic.   Black Americans see themselves
foremost as very American and very unfairly treated.   In
addition, they are likable, determined to succeed, smart,
intelligent, and hardworking.   They also see their own
group as fairly aggressive and violent, and not fully
trustworthy.   Their views of other groups are similarly
balanced with good and less good attributes. Violence is
apparently very salient in their judgments of themselves
and others, and they see blacks as no more aggressive and
violent than Mexican, Puerto Rican, or Albanian Americans,
and as even less aggressive and violent than white
Americans. At the same time, white Americans are viewed as
being   particularly powerful as well as very American,
making white and black groups much alike except for
differences in power and its implications in terms of
unfair treatment of blacks.

In general, blacks hold basically favorable views of
other ethnic groups, although tempered with particular
shortcomings, and they rate themselves similarly,
suggesting to us that they do not feel the need to put
other groups down in the process of keeping self-respect.
They do seem to realize that certain other ethnic groups

are especially favorable towards blacks (e.g., the Polish Americans and the middle-class whites) and in these instances they contribute to a solid, mutual respect and appreciation.   They also sense which groups are racist or at least anti-black (e.g., the working-class whites and the Arab and Albanian parents), but they do not reciprocate particularly hostile sentiments in return.   As a group, then, the black American parents appear to be realistic, accepting, and charitable towards various ethnic groups, which makes their social attitudes much like those of the middle-class white and the Polish Americans, the two groups with most power and privilege in the two communities studied.

This similarity between the values of our black parents and the white middle-class group is evident when measured by the Kluckhohn scales.   The close black-white alignment of values suggests to us that whatever the mainstream American value profile or the American philosophy of life might be, blacks have as much of a hand in its shape as mainstream whites do.   In terms of the values measured here, blacks are similar to the more privileged whites and dissimilar to other ethnic groups whose values or social attitudes deviate from certain "American" standards.   For instance, the Arab Americans place a great deal of stress on staying close to one's family and seeking a secure place of work in a large organization, Arab and Albanian parents question the worth of coeducational schooling, and working-class whites question the worth of racially or ethnically mixed schooling.   In these instances the black parents' values, like those of the middle-class whites, are clearly different.

This similarity of perspectives of black and middle-class white Americans parallels closely the findings of Lorand Szalay who discovered that the "psychocultural distance between black and white Americans was relatively narrow, compared with the distance between Latin American immigrants and both groups" (Cunningham, 1984).   The present findings, however, indicate that there may be critical differences among white subgroups: we have found a substantial "psychocultural distance" between blacks and working-class white parents.

The black parents' views on the essentials of curriculum content for their children's schooling is also consonant with all other ethnic groups except for that of working-class whites who question the need for certain subjects such as English language arts or histories of other ethnic groups. They also are similar to other groups in their outlooks for their children's occupational future; they would love to have their children attain positions in the top professions and they are optimistic that they can at least become skilled workers in the world of work, although, unlike the white middle-class parents, they realize that the chances of success are very limited. Thus, any work at all is tolerated by the black parents, even though they are not delighted with that prospect. In summary, blacks show themselves to be strong allies of multiculturalism. They are sympathetic to other ethnic minorities, whom they regard as people like themselves who have their own precious culture and language styles to preserve. In their attitudes and beliefs, they appear to be as much shapers and contributors to the "American way of life" as any other American subgroup. Finally, their perspectives on social issues that touch the lives of minority groups are in no fundamental way hostile or discordant to the wishes of any other ethnic group, minority or mainstream.

Table 6.1

Responses of Black American Respondents
Regarding Assimilation and Culture Maintenance*

Culture Maintenance Arguments:

	Pontiac Black Respondents	Hamtramck Black Respondents
Arguments Against		
All people living in America will not have a common base for understanding each other	3.67	3.52
There will be different languages and cultural standards throughout America	6.00	4.85
America will be divided into segregated units	4.17	3.15
Arguments For		
People will be allowed to express an important part of their identity	6.42	5.44
People will feel secure in their group identity, and this will make them open and sympathetic to other groups	6.16	4.97
The nation can keep the best that different cultural and racial groups have to offer	6.12	5.27

Assimilation Arguments:

	Pontiac Black Respondents	Hamtramck Black Respondents
Arguments For		
All people living in America will have a common base for understanding each other	3.47	3.45
The same language and cultural standards will exist for all Americans	3.63	3.33
America will be unified and cohesive	2.69	3.02
Arguments Against		
People will be robbed of a very important part of their personal identity	6.19	4.60
People will have been forced to give up something valuable, and this will make them hostile toward others	6.16	4.62
The nation loses the best that different cultural and racial groups have to offer	5.93	4.64

DISAGREE   1 (Definitely)   2   3   4 (Neutral)   5   6   7 (Definitely)   AGREE

* Data analyzed by means of Kruskal-Wallis Chi Square. Connecting bars indicate statistical significance at one percent level of confidence.

Table 6.2

Mean Scores for Black Respondents
Regarding Retention of the Heritage Culture*

In your opinion, how far should your own group go in maintaining its culture and traditions?	Hamtramck Black Respondents	Pontiac Black Respondents
1. Step A: Since our culture and traditions are not American, they should not be maintained.	2.93	3.26
2. Step B: Keep our own cultural styles of foods, dress, songs and dances.	6.40	5.87
3. Step C: Keep our own cultural values, such as how children should behave with parents, husbands with wives, dating practices, etc.	6.14	5.76
4. Step D: Attend courses about our own cultural history and traditions, not in public schools but in church-run or community-run classes.	5.63	4.79
5. Step E: Have courses about our own cultural history and traditions taught in public schools.	5.28	5.55
6. Step F: Have equal time in schools spent on our own cultural history and traditions as on American history & traditions.	5.21	5.47

DISAGREE   1____2____3____4____5____6____7   AGREE
            Definitely   Neutral   Definitely

---

* Data analyzed by means of Kruskal-Wallis Chi Square. Connecting bars indicate statistical significance at one percent level of confidence.

149

Table 6.3

Mean Scores for Black Respondents
Regarding the Maintenance of the Heritage Language*

In your opinion, how far should your own group go in using its its own language?	Hamtramck Black Respondents	Pontiac Black Respondents
1. Step A: Cultural groups whose language is not Standard English should never use own language.	1.86	2.46
2. Step B: Use our own language for festival days, cultural songs, traditional stories, prayers and religious services.	5.76	5.32
3. Step C: Use our own language for speaking with older family members, like grandparents.	5.43	5.38
4. Step D: Use our own language for most or all speaking within the family.	5.37	5.11
5. Step E: Learn to read and write our own language not through school, but through church-run or community-run classes.	5.42 ⌞_____⌟	3.97
6. Step F: Use own language for part of the teaching and learning in public schools.	4.59	3.86
7. Step G: Give equal time in schools to the use of own language as to Standard English.	3.88	4.19

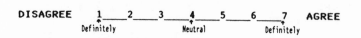

DISAGREE   1____2____3____4____5____6____7   AGREE
           Definitely   Neutral   Definitely

* Data analyzed by means of Kruskal-Wallis Chi Square.
  Connecting bars indicate statistical significance at one
  percent level of confidence.

Table 6.4

Mean Scores Regarding the Consequences of Bidialectism*

Would they:	Black Parent Respondents in Pontiac			Black Parent Respondents in Hamtramck		
	If your son/daughter were bidialectal	If your son/daughter spoke only Black English	If your son/daughter spoke only Standard English	If your son/daughter were bidialectal	If your son/daughter spoke only Black English	If your son/daughter spoke only Standard English
1. feel accepted in America?	5.69	3.72	5.44	5.77	3.19	5.63
2. feel a sense of pride?	6.10	4.08	5.26	5.88	4.21	4.93
3. make their parents happy?	6.18	4.38	5.23	6.23	3.67	5.21
4. feel open and relaxed with others?	6.00	3.26	4.77	5.86	2.95	5.23
5. bring status and respect to their group?	5.90	3.87	4.66	5.54	3.47	4.16
6. stand out as different?	4.26	4.92	3.97	5.54	3.47	4.16
7. be treated like second-class citizens?	4.16	4.53	4.03	2.65	4.44	2.74
8. get good marks in school?	6.16	2.87	5.24	5.12	2.28	4.72
9. have a chance for certain jobs others can't get?	6.21	3.45	5.11	4.95	3.67	4.23
10. be sympathetic to people?	5.47	4.32	4.58	4.65	3.84	4.07
11. show intelligence?	5.37	3.66	4.39	5.16	3.09	4.40

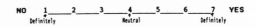

NO 1____2____3____4____5____6____7 YES
    Definitely   Neutral   Definitely

---

* Data analyzed by means of Wilcoxon sign-ranks test. Connecting bars indicate statistical significance at one percent level of confidence.

151

Table 6.5

Mean Attribution Ratings-of Own Groups and Other Groups*

How ..... are	Black Parent Respondents in Pontiac				Black Parent Respondents in Hamtramck			
	most Puerto Rican Americans	most Mexican Americans	most Black Americans	most White Americans	most Polish Americans	most Arab Americans	most Albanian Americans	most Black Americans
1. hardworking	4.91	4.79	5.53	5.08	5.71	4.91	4.54	5.05
2. aggressive or violent	4.61	4.52	4.46	5.51	3.69	4.38	4.83	4.88
3. American	4.46	4.49	5.45	5.44	4.61	3.35	3.33	6.21
4. likely to stick together as a group	5.82	5.77	4.59	5.80	6.23	6.44	6.35	5.00
5. powerful	2.60	2.65	4.03	6.43	4.35	3.93	3.48	4.35
6. similar to me	4.12	4.06	5.63	4.37	1.86	2.05	1.86	5.47
7. intelligent at school	4.27	4.49	5.13	5.49	4.88	4.17	4.00	5.14
8. smart with practical things	4.70	4.49	5.67	5.34	5.05	4.07	4.31	5.70
9. trustworthy	3.55	3.64	4.13	3.78	3.74	2.91	3.81	5.60
10. law abiding (good citizen)	3.91	3.82	4.26	4.29	4.84	3.88	3.86	4.86
11. unfairly treated	4.88	4.97	5.54	2.53	2.14	2.98	3.05	5.95
12. likable	4.31	4.59	5.30	4.59	4.50	3.15	3.23	5.43

NOT AT ALL 1 2 3 4 5 6 7 VERY
Definitely   Neutral   Definitely

* Data analyzed by means of Kruskal-Wallis Chi Square. Connecting bars indicate statistical significance at one percent level of confidence.

Table 6.6

Mean Social Distance Ratings in Pontiac and Hamtramck*

How willing are you personally to accept these people?	Black Parent Respondents in Pontiac				Black Parent Respondents in Hamtramck			
	most Puerto Rican Americans	most Mexican Americans	most Black Americans	most White Americans	most Polish Americans	most Arab Americans	most Albanian Americans	most Black Americans
1. As a family member through marriage?	4.81	4.42	6.58	4.34	3.30	2.54	2.51	6.47
2. As a close personal friend?	5.19	5.24	6.26	5.21	4.63	3.33	3.23	6.19
3. As a close neighbor in my neighborhood or apartment building?	5.51	5.58	6.18	5.71	5.54	3.91	3.58	6.05
4. As a co-worker or partner at work?	6.03	6.05	6.51	6.16	5.72	4.61	4.47	6.02
5. As a citizen of the U.S.A.?	6.08	6.10	6.66	6.36	5.79	4.84	4.81	6.49

NOT AT ALL 1 Definitely 2 3 4 Neutral 5 6 7 Definitely VERY

* Data analyzed by means of Wilcoxon sign-ranks test. Connecting bars indicate statistical significance at one percent level of confidence.

153

Table 6.7

Mean Scores for Black Respondents
Regarding Basic Values*

	Hamtramck Black Respondents	Pontiac Black Respondents
1. All a person should want out of life in the way of a career is a secure, not too.....	3.35	3.25
2. When people are born, the success they are going to have is already in the cards....	2.05	2.67
3. The secret of happiness is not expecting too much out of life and being content...	2.77	2.85
4. Nothing is worth the sacrifice of moving away from one's parents.....	2.12	2.00
5. The best kind of job to have is one where you are part of an organization.....	2.93	2.95
6. Planning only makes a person unhappy since your plans hardly ever.....	2.12	2.05
7. Nowadays with world conditions the way they are, the wise person lives for today......	4.40	3.40

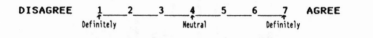

DISAGREE   1___2___3___4___5___6___7   AGREE

Definitely   Neutral   Definitely

* Data analyzed by means of Kruskal-Wallis Chi Square. Connecting bars indicate statistical significance at one percent level of confidence.

Table 6.8

Mean Scores for Black Respondents
Regarding Education*

	Hamtramck Black Respondents	Pontiac Black Respondents
1. The future is bright for young people.	4.49	4.47
2. Education is more important today than past.	6.43	6.42
3. Education would be better if boys and girls separated.	2.02	2.72
4. Schools should not have dances.	2.21	2.67
5. Schools should have a racial mix of children.	6.02	6.35
6. Children should be taught more discipline in school.	5.79	5.85
7. Teachers are not as devoted to students as in past.	5.49	5.12
8. High school graduation isn't enough.	6.07	6.42
9. Students aren't as interested in learning as in past.	5.54	5.40
10. Parents don't show enough interest in children's education.	5.58	5.42
11. Schools don't give enough say to parents.	5.00	3.72

DISAGREE 1____2____3____4____5____6____7 AGREE
          Definitely   Neutral   Definitely

* Data analyzed by means of Kruskal-Wallis Chi Square.
  Connecting bars indicate statistical significance at one
  percent level of confidence.

155

Table 6.9

Mean Scores for Black Respondents
Regarding School Subjects*

	Hamtramck Black Respondents	Pontiac Black Respondents
1. English language arts	6.58	6.85
2. Language arts for own language	5.51	5.31
3. Language arts for another language	5.19	5.51
4. Mathematics	6.91	6.78
5. Science	6.14	6.50
6. Computers	6.70	6.49
7. American history	5.54	6.30
8. History of own group	6.47	6.28
9. History of other groups	5.47	5.60
10. Music	5.16	5.05
11. Physical education	6.09	5.53
12. Hygiene and health	6.72	6.70
13. Sex education	5.79	5.59
14. Practical/technical training	6.49	6.18

UNIMPORTANT 1____2____3____4____5____6____7 IMPORTANT
              Definitely   Neutral   Definitely

---

* Data analyzed by means of Kruskal-Wallis Chi Square. Connecting bars
indicate statistical significance at one percent level of confidence.

156

Table 6.10

Mean Scores for Black Respondents
Regarding the Desirability and Likelihood of Employment Prospects*

	How happy would you be if your son/ daughter became.....		What are the chances of your son/daughter becoming.....	
	Hamtramck Black Respondents	Pontiac Black Respondents	Hamtramck Black Respondents	Pontiac Black Respondents
1. a lawyer, a doctor, a director of a large company, etc. (a major professional position)?	6.65	6.50	4.98	5.07
2. an owner of a small business, small restaurant, a bookkeeper, (a minor professional position)?	6.21	6.15	4.95	5.10
3. a machinist, roofer, plumber, nurse, secretary (a skilled worker position)?	6.17	5.62	5.21	5.57
4. a road repair man, gas station attendant, a file clerk (a semiskilled worker position)?	5.29	4.77	4.50	4.85
5. a daily laborer in a factory or on a construction project, a house cleaner (an unskilled worker position)?	4.31	3.35	4.62	4.37

UNHAPPY 1___2___3___4___5___6___7 HAPPY
           Definitely   Neutral   Definitely

CHANCES
POOR   1___2___3___4___5___6___7 GOOD
           Definitely   Neutral   Definitely

* Data analyzed by means of Kruskal-Wallis Chi Square. Connecting bars indicate statistical significance at one percent level of confidence.

157

7

Two Faces of Multiculturalism: Sobering Reflections and Exciting Possibilities!

In this final chapter we have three goals in mind. One aim is to draw out major themes that emerge from the investigation and speak briefly about their social significance. However, because the themes were derived from the way we collected the data, it is obligatory that we emphasize again the limitations we see on the research side of the study so that readers will realize the risks involved in over-generalizing our findings. A second aim is to explore the area just beyond the bounds of this study, that is, the area where the wishes and desires of parents are translated into action and implementation. On this topic, we have some preliminary data to suggest that ethnic groups differ fundamentally in the ways they go about putting their expressed desires for multiculturalism in America into practice, not only in their own lives, but also, indirectly, in the lives of their children. Some of these differences in implementation are traceable to palpable issues such as time of residence in the United States. But even when we explore the effects of residence time, certain groups do not act as one might predict. As a consequence, our scratching the surface of this topic makes very evident the need for more detailed, tightly focused study of generational changes in attitudes towards assimilation and multiculturalism, and of the creative modes some ethnic groups utilize to achieve their objectives. Finally, a third aim is to take the implementation issue one step further by describing a particular ethnic group's attempts to keep its heritage culture and language alive by offering their children as research subjects in a school system project in which their children are instructed, half-time, in their heritage language. That this project is conducted in a public school setting and that it is given equal time to that given conventional English language schooling is particularly interesting to us.

LIMITATIONS OF OUR STUDY

All research in the social or behavioral sciences runs the risk of not being much more exact and, very likely, much less interesting to read than a skillful journalist's analysis of the same social events. Scientific procedures are slow, detailed, boring approaches to social happenings, but, we believe, they are necessary if one wants to reduce personal interpretations and unconscious biases so that the happenings can be better understood. In this investigation, we simply wanted to take the "attitudinal" pulse of urban Americans on a fundamental American dilemma, namely, letting ethnics be themselves versus helping them to become American. From our first encounters with the informants for this study, we bypassed the fascinating stories each of them could have told us and concentrated on their reactions, measured in terms of rating scales, to a programmed set of questions so selected as to represent all possible points of view about a number of issues we believed to be socially important. This empirical pulse taking permits us to make a number of new, extremely thought-provoking, and, in many respects, unanticipated conclusions. But we have reservations about the shortcomings of our research that need to be reviewed in order to put these conclusions in a reasonable perspective. This is a single research investigation only, and the issues it addresses deserve many such studies. Thus, it should be considered at best as an exploratory, pilot investigation.

In the first place, our attempt to describe intergroup relations as they actually are in one urban center meant that we concentrated on the prominent, large ethnic groups that exist there. Although our coverage is broad compared to most social-psychological studies, we nonetheless realize that we should not be overly confident of the outcomes. We describe certain major groups, but other smaller ethnic groups were not included, for example the Vietnamese, the Laotians, and the Ukrainians, and many others that also contribute to life in the communities surveyed. Furthermore, the results we have are based on a particular selection of ethnic groups (Polish, Arab, Albanian, Puerto Rican, Mexican, black and white Americans) and because we have found basic differences in the reactions of these groups, there is no grounds at all for generalizing to Portuguese, Italian, Cuban, Hungarian Americans that would be encountered in other settings. So there is a group selection limitation clearly built into our study.

Second, although we arranged it so that our selection of informants could be interviewed (not asked to fill out questionnaires) in their homes through their most comfortable language, we had to keep small the size of the samples of people chosen to be the representatives of particular ethnic groups. So there is a sample size limitation involved here as well, and even though we felt comfortable choosing random samples of families from each ethnic community, it was not a case of a city-wide randomization but merely one involving ethnic lists provided by the schools.

Third, it would have been valuable had we selected equal numbers of mothers and fathers for each sample, but we were limited by cultural factors (e.g., that for certain groups it was appropriate for fathers only to speak for the family, or in other cases, because so few fathers were available, mothers were the spokespersons. So we have the reactions of "heads of households" not both parents.

Fourth, we felt that those doing the interviewing should be of the same ethnicity and language background as the respondents, and for certain groups this was absolutely necessary. Correct as this choice may seem, we realized that the "co-ethnicity" factor could have a biasing effect by amplifying the emotional sense of ethnicity and within-group solidarity and thereby unintentionally promoting the multicultural option over the assimilation option. We have no way to gauge how much this factor biased our findings.

Finally, we were not able to adequately treat generational changes that very likely transpire as families reside in the United States over long periods of time. To do so would have involved complicated sampling (e.g., subgroups within each ethnic group with short, medium, and long residence periods). Thus, in this regard, the exploratory nature of our study will be very evident when in the next section we attempt to use the data at hand to interpret the effects of time of residence in the United States.

None of these limitations is insurmountable, and hopefully, future studies will profit from our list of the shortcomings of the present study. Nonetheless, because of these limitations, the general themes and trends we present below should be considered more as hypotheses for future research attempts than as definitive or generalizable conclusions.

THE MAJOR RESULTS OF OUR STUDY

Despite a host of differences in attitudes and perspectives among the various groups included in the study, there is a surprising degree of consensus and agreement favoring the pro-multiculturalism side of the assimilation versus multiculturalism debate.   This means that there was just as strong a concensus against the assimilation side.   Not only is it the immigrant ethnic groups that are so favorable towards the multicultural alternative--the working class samples of Polish, Arab, Albanian, Puerto Rican, and Mexican American parents--but an established American ethnic minority, the working class blacks, also clearly favors the multicultural option their own group as well as for other ethnic groups. Likewise, the established, middle class whites also favor the multicultural option over assimilation, and even our sample of working class whites turned out to be at least neutral on the basic debate issue. Are we dealing with a case of response bias here? We do not think so because of the consistency of responses we found when arguments both for and against each alternative were presented to our respondents.

A legitimate question then comes to mind: Where are those Americans who do support the assimilation option? There certainly are such people out there. We have no adequate response to this question. We tried our best to encourage expression of pro-assimilation sentiments if they were actually felt, but we failed to uncover trends in that

direction.   One possibility is that this study dealt only
with working-class parental groups, with the exception of
the middle-class white group.   Might it be that members of
immigrant ethnic groups who have arrived at middle-class
status positions in the United States are the pro-
assimilationists that our study missed?   They are the ones
referred to in popular American stories that tell of
grandparents or parents who left the old country with the
vow to put the old culture and language away and to become
American.   And the success of these older generations is
used as proof of the assimilation ideal.   Incidentally, it
is interesting to speculate about these models of success:
if they came to America as teenagers or older, they would
very likely have been highly skilled bicultural bilinguals!

One possible interpretation for this extensive
endorsement of the multiculturalism alternative is that
conventional wisdom about assimilation being a fundamental
American ideal may be out of date or wrong.   A single
exploratory study like ours cannot in itself be persuasive
on this point, but at least we can now raise some important
questions about American ideals and the people who champion
them.   For instance, we have found that black Americans,
even those from less privileged social class backgrounds,
appear to be co-shapers or co-contributors to the "American
way of life" that supposedly makes the assimilation process
one of its ideals.   And yet we find that blacks appear to
be as much in the vanguard as more privileged whites in
supporting the opportunities for ethnic groups to maintain
their ethnic identities.

Our study also brings to light the possibility that
established Americans, white or black, may not be the only
or the main trendsetters for a possible change in the ideal
of assimilation.   Rather, demographic changes in the United
States in the form of large subpopulations of particular
ethnic groups, provide opportunities and encouragement for
each group to maintain its identity.   Consequently, it is
feasible now to maintain one's ethnicity and still be as
American as anyone else.   However, the major finding
uncovered in our study is that none of the groups surveyed-
-the immigrant ethnic groups nor the ethnic minority
blacks--wanted to give up their heritage culture in order
to become Americanized but instead wanted to add a second
culture and in most cases a second language or dialect.
Thus, a central idea that emerges is that ethnic minorities
no longer feel forced to make a choice between culture
maintenance and assimilation, but rather prefer to take a

third alternative, namely develop full-scale biculturality and bilinguality.   Stated otherwise, they seem to want their family members to become "double breeds" rather than single breeds or half-breeds, and "bilinguals" rather than semi-bilinguals or monolinguals. The decision then is not a choice between one culture or another, but the adoption of two cultures rather than one, with nothing lost in the process. There was also very strong agreement, found with all groups surveyed, that maintaining only the heritage culture or only the heritage language would be unmistakably dysfunctional and undesirable, and that bilinguality was better than English-only monolinguality.

When asked how far groups should go to protect and maintain heritage cultures and languages, consistent and clear group differences emerged. Keeping heritage cultures and languages vital in the home and, thus, across generations was solidly accepted not only by immigrant ethnic groups, but also by the black ethnic minority group, and by the middle-class white majority group. Support was even given to inculcating distinctive ethnic values through the socialization process (e.g., how children should be raised).   However, group differences emerged around the issue of bringing ethnicity outside the home and the ethnic community and into the public domain.   Teaching about heritage cultures and languages in community- or church-based classes was perfectly acceptable to certain ethnic groups (e.g., Mexican and Polish Americans) but much less so to other groups (e.g., Puerto Rican Americans) who expressed the wish to have public schools definitely involved.   Going public with heritage cultures and languages was unmistakably favored by Arab and Puerto Rican American groups, but this step was beyond the acceptable range for the otherwise very supportive middle-class white group.   Thus, we have uncovered potentially instructive group differences about where the boundaries of acceptability for expansion of multiculturalism should be, boundaries that are immediately transformed into limits of tolerance.

Although these boundaries vary, all groups of parents surveyed, with no exception, strongly support the development and fostering of bilingualism for their own children, whether that would involve the heritage language of the group plus English, or, in the case of anglophones, English plus another foreign language (which boils down to some other ethnic group's heritage language).   This extensive and strong support for bilingualism is particularly interesting because in the minds of the parents interviewed, it means something more than keeping an ethnic and a linguistic identity alive. It also means that young people nowadays will profit from being bilingual not only in their educational pursuits, but also in the world of work where being able to communicate with other ethnic groups has become a very valuable asset. This finding also suggests that another basic American ideal, that of having everyone "speak American" or "speak white", may be changing.

Our findings in the domain of intergroup attitudes provoke upset and concern, a much more serious matter than that suggested in a recent New York Times editorial. That editorial, entitled "Happy Lief Ericson Day", relates the longstanding tug of war between Columbus fans and Ericson fans, including some fourteen million Scandinavian Americans, and is treated humorously and lightly. Some one hundred years ago, Yankees in Massachusetts provoked local Italians (who were preparing for the four hundredth anniversary of 1492), by erecting a monument to Ericson in Boston. Fifty years later, Columbus fans put up a statue of Columbus at the Minnesota State Capitol. Last year, the governor of Minnesota issued a proclamation for Ericson Day but none for Columbus Day. And President Reagan issued proclamations for both days! The key comment about all this was: "Competing ethnic pride is as American as the melting pot" (New York Times, October 8, 1988).

Our findings on intergroup attitudes and the "competing ethnic prides" in the greater Detroit area are anything but humorous because certain ethnic groups are demonstrably the target of widespread prejudice and hate, and many of the groups surveyed express disdain and suspicion of all groups but their own. We expected to find "normal" degrees of ethnocentrism, for example that members of most ethnic group would have a favorable own-group image and would prefer that marital partners be chosen from among "their own kind". It is another thing to uncover a number of instances of affective segregation of own-group from all other ethnic groups in the community. This form of ethnic isolation was particularly apparent in the attitude profiles of immigrant ethnic groups; Arab and Albanian groups in Hamtramck showed little appreciation for one another, and Puerto Rican and Mexican groups in Pontiac mutually distanced themselves from one another in terms of the attributions assigned and in terms of social distance placements. In general, "white Americans" received more

favorable reactions from other groups and they were seen as
the most "powerful", the most "American", and the least
"unfairly treated" group of all.   But "black Americans"
were seriously downgraded by many parental groups and kept
far away in terms of social distance ratings.   One might
have suspected that groups related through a common
language and pan-cultural tradition—the Puerto Rican and
Mexican Americans—would show some form of mutual sympathy
and appreciation.   We found, instead, a mutual neutrality
of attitudes bordering on distrust and a view of the other
group as definitely "not similar to us".   Certain groups
were more charitable in their attitudes towards others,
notably the black parents, the white middle-class group and
the Polish Americans. At the same time, our white working-
class group was outright racist towards blacks in
particular, and hostile and distrustful towards immigrant
ethnics in general. Thus, it is clear from our study that
ethnic tensions and disharmony mark the lives of all
members of this community, and that ethnic groups
themselves contribute strongly to these ethnic tensions.

These data on intergroup attitude networks are
critically important to the viability of a social policy of
multiculturalism.   Richard Lambert has clearly recognized
and documented the increasingly conflictual nature of
ethnic and racial relations in the United States,the
escalation of "ethnic specificity", and the "direction of
violence" in American intergroup relations (Lambert, 1981).
Lambert sends the message that not only are these relations
dangerous but they are also essentially out of control.   A
policy of multiculturalism cannot succeed in an attitudinal
atmosphere of mutual distrust and suspicion, exaggerated
ethnocentrism, and own-group isolation.   To argue that
"competing ethnic pride" is to be expected or that it is a
light weight matter that can best be held in check through
a policy of assimilation is to avoid facing much deeper
issues.

An alternative approach is to capitalize on one
incidental finding of our study and to move on from there.
The finding of importance is that the groups in our study
who were most secure, both economically and ethnically—the
middle-class whites and the established working-class
Polish Americans in Hamtramck—were also the most open and
charitable in their views of other ethnic groups.   On the
other hand, the ethnically secure but economically insecure
blacks were also generally favorable towards other ethnic
groups.   This suggests to us that a sense of security, in

one form or another, may be a pivotal factor. A
constructive next step would be to design ways to insure
and increase a sense of ethnic security for all groups.
Helping all groups to realize that they share a common fate
might generate an appreciation for other groups' attempts
to guard their identities.   Thus, perhaps a security
around one's own ethnic identity could orient thinking away
from own-group concerns to the concerns of others. Some
research is now underway on this constructive alternative,
and the development of this line of inquiry could be
invaluable to real-life applications of either
multicultural or assimilationist policies (see Berry,
Kalin, & Taylor, 1977 and Lambert, Mermigis, & Taylor,
1986). The main point here is that behavioral scientists
may now be the best equipped to do something useful about
groups in conflict by first conducting research on socially
significant topics and then by taking such research into
the realm of action directed toward ameliorating community
relations.

Putting Desires for Multiculturalism into Practice

Up to now we have been dealing mainly with the complex
feelings and attitudes of parents, the stands they take on
dealing with policies about culture and language
maintenance, their desires and aspirations for the
continuity or discontinuity of heritage traditions and
languages, and their perspectives on how ethnic families
might best adjust to American values and the language of
America. In this section, our purpose is to explore, as
far as our data permit, how these different ethnic
minority groups put their policies into practice. For one
thing, we want to see if these parents serve as models for
their children in terms of maintaining a heritage culture
and language while developing skills in the American
culture and language. Since we have found that most
immigrant ethnic groups expect their children to juggle
the two and become fully bicultural and bilingual, it is
reasonable to ask if parents set an example of culture
balancing or whether they shift the responsibility for
biculturality off to their children. It could be that
parents have the hardest time and are unable either to keep
the heritage culture alive or pick up the new culture.
Perhaps both tasks are so demanding that they effectively
fail at both.
The element of time, specifically residence time in

the new land, becomes a critical factor at this point in
the discussion because it could have various, quite
contradictory, effects. For instance, time in the new
setting could work against culture maintenance, or it
could provide the necessary opportunities for parents to
become fully bicultural and bilingual, or it could even be
used by families to withdraw from the real world and lock
themselves into the "old world" culture and the old world
language. In order to appreciate the role of time, we
present in Table 7.1 the average number of years each of
our group has lived in the United States.

The basic question we ask is: How well have these
apparently highly motivated parents done in passing on the
heritage culture and language to their own children? How
receptive are the children?

**Parents' Fluency in the Heritage Language and in
English**

During the interviews, parents were asked to rate
themselves in terms of their fluency in their heritage
language and in English. The average self-ratings are
presented in Table 7.2. Considered from a societal point
of view, it is interesting to note that four of the five
ethnic newcomer groups to America--the Arab, Albanian,
Puerto Rican and Mexican Americans--report that they have
very strong skills in their heritage languages. What is
striking is the fact that these four groups of ethnic
newcomer adults have kept these languages alive over
varying years of residence in the United States. Then,
looking more closely, we find no systematic relation for
these four groups of parents between time in the United
States and loss of heritage language. In fact, although
more than 50 percent of the Arabic Americans have been in
the United States for 10 to 25 years, 98 percent rate their
skills in Arabic at the native fluency point on our scales.
Similarly, over 53 percent of the Albanian American
parents have been in the United States for 12 to 16 years,
yet some 90 percent of them have "native" or "native-like"
skills in Albanian. The figures for Puerto Ricans are:
over 50 percent in the United States for 10 - 30 years and
95 percent have native skills in Spanish; for Mexican
Americans, over 50 percent have lived in the United States
for over 40 years and still over 75 percent have native or
near native skills in Spanish. This means that four of
the five ethnic immigrant groups of parents in our study

show no signs of heritage language attrition over, in some cases, very long periods of residency in the United States.

There are several ways of interpreting these outcomes and each has   important social implications. First, one can consider these trends as the development of a bank of foreign language resources for the nation as a whole, if our small sample of five ethnolinguistic minority groups in one urban center is any indication of what would likely be found throughout the nation. Here we find large proportions of four of the five groups of parents surveyed who have kept up native or near native-like control of Arabic, Albanian, and two cultural forms of Spanish. Maintaining the languages in these cases also means introducing younger family members to the languages and cultures, or at least developing children's skills of understanding the spoken language.

Second, these findings call into question the anticipated effects of assimilation that are normally associated with the American melting pot theory. Contrary to expectations, there may be more resistance to the assimilation process than one might expect, at least for the parent generation.

A third interpretation raises the question of the price ethnolinguistic minority group parents pay when they resist linguistic and cultural assimilation in this fashion. From a societal perspective, it appears to be difficult to develop maximum skills in English when the heritage language is maintained. The Arab, Puerto Rican, and Albanian American parents rate themselves as decidedly poorer in English than in the heritage language by a factor of two full scale positions on our seven point rating scales (see Table 7.2). Mainstream Americans might well ask questions about this discrepancy, arguing that minority language families jeopardize their own and their children's chances of advancement in the United States if deficits in English language skills are not surmounted. However, the Mexican American parents appear to have met this challenge since they rate themselves as equally skilled in Spanish and English. Keeping in mind that the Mexican American parents have been in the United States for the longest period of time of any group (see Table 7.1), their binguality suggests that, with time or in spite of time, the language balancing act can be carried off successfully. But it could be argued that its success has required continuous input, through immigration, of new waves of Mexican Americans.

The Polish American parent group is of interest because it is the one exception among our five language minority groups. Polish is not maintained at a level comparable to that of the other four groups, and although English is relatively stronger than Polish, it is not, on the average, considered native-like. On the surface, this might be interpreted as an example of a group being caught between two cultures or two cultural sources of influence, leaving them with nonnative-like control of both languages. Actually, on closer analysis we find two separate subgroups who contribute to the overall average: those in our Polish sample who have been in the United States for a short period of time (1 - 3 years) have not developed full skills in English, but are strong in Polish, whereas those here for ten years or more have native-like skills in English, but have not kept up Polish. Thus, one way to master English is to <u>not</u> use the heritage language, but, as the Mexican Americans demonstrate, that is not the <u>only</u> way.

Clearly, language minority groups receive different degrees of social pressure to maintain heritage languages and/or to master the national language. Time of residence in the United States seems to promote full Spanish-English bilingualism for the Mexican Americans while for the Polish Americans it promotes English at the expense of Polish. It is difficult to predict whether more time of United States residency will lead the Arab, Puerto Rican and Albanian American parents, who have been here for nine to twelve years only, down the Mexican American or down the Polish American route. One thing we now know, though, is that time of residency in the United States is not the only factor involved in the final outcome; nor does time of United States residency necessarily lead to linguistic assimilation among the parent generation.

Children's Fluency in the Heritage Language and in English

Surprised as we are to learn that the majority of our parental groups keep their heritage languages alive, it still could be that the story essentially ends with the parents. Will their children, the upcoming generation, pick up the linguistic torch? Certainly, they will have lived with parents who speak heritage languages, but there is no guarantee that the language will actually be learned

and used.   It often happens that the   parents live out
their lives with the culture and language of the old
country   while the offspring go off on a new cultural and
linguistic tangent.   The   data in Table 7.2 throw some
interesting light on these possibilities.   Apparently
three of our groups--the Arab, Puerto Rican, and Albanian
Americans--are able to relay the heritage language to their
children so that   the latter are as native-like in the
heritage language as their parents.   In   addition, the
children appear to have surpassed their parents by
developing higher-level skills in English.   Since we
already know that the aim of all   five ethnolinguistic
groups was to provide for full bilingual and bicultural
competence for their children, it seems that in these three
cases, the wishes   of the parents have been satisfied.   We
presume that skill in the heritage language has been
thoroughly rooted in the home while English has
simultaneously been brought up to native-like or near
native-like levels through the school and through contacts
outside the home.   These outside-the-home   influences are
the likely catalysts that permit the children to surpass
the   parents in English.

These three cases throw new light on the assimilation
process: assimilation need not entail the eradication of
heritage languages and   cultures.   Instead, the
assimilation process can run its course at the same   time
as a new language and culture are added, without
necessarily replacing   the old with the new.   If the
"replacement" effects of assimilation can be   avoided, then
the second or third generation can more easily and more
comfortably become bilingual and bicultural than can the
first.

At the same time, we have other data from the Mexican
and Polish American   families that are intriguing because
they tell a different story.   Of all   five groups surveyed,
these two   have been in the United States for the   longest
periods of time (see Table 7.1), and we find that children
in these   families have very limited skills in their
heritage languages and very strong   skills in English.
Furthermore, in Mexican and Polish American families that
have been here relatively few years, the children's
heritage language   skills are much stronger than is the
case for families with longer years of   residence.   In the
latter case, the children's command of the heritage
language has nearly disappeared.   Thus, some
ethnolinguistic groups do show   the replacement or

eradication effects of linguistic assimilation just as clearly as other groups resist those effects by developing full bilingual abilities. A limitation of our study is that we have nothing further to say about factors within the family or outside the family that account for these very pronounced differences.

Various questions come to mind. Will new generations of Arab, Puerto Rican, and Albanian American children go the way of the Mexican and Polish American children when their families have been in residence in the United States for twenty or thirty years? After some ten years of residency, the parents of these three groups have kept the heritage language strong and so have their children. But will new generations of Arab, Puerto Rican, or Albanian American parents keep these skills over a twenty or thirty year period, i.e., the time span for the Mexican and Polish American families in our study? One could argue that there is no need to lose the heritage language through generations in the United States if that language is well rooted in childhood by native-speaking parents and if there are societal props to make the language valuable. Thus the Arab American families may place great importance on the heritage language because it is essential for the services and liturgy of a world-wide religion that itself forms an essential aspect of the Arabic culture. In a similar fashion, Puerto Rican American families may argue that while they are American in all respects, they also happen to be Hispanic and thus they have democratic rights to maintain Spanish and still be accepted as Americans. From this point of view, Arabic and Spanish could survive generations of residence. Albanian American families could be motivated to keep their language and culture alive because, as many of our informants maintain, they and their children will return home as soon as they are financially able. This may or may not be a realistic rationale and one might wonder whether this form of motivation will be as durable and effective through generations as that expressed by Arab and Puerto Rican families.

The Mexican and Polish American cases are more puzzling. Why do these parents who show such a strong desire to maintain culture and language and to foster bilinguality for their children, not keep the language alive over generations or, in the case of the Polish parents, even within their own generation? Apparently, they permit English to dominate in their children's lives at the expense of Spanish and Polish. Is it these

particular parental   groups who give up on the heritage
language, or is it these particular ethnic   groups of
children who are under especially strong pressure to become
"American" and to erase traces of foreignness? Could it be
that because the Polish and Mexican American parents were
so skilled in English that they provided too much of a
temptation to their children to turn to English at home
rather than the heritage language? If this is so, then the
Arab, Albanian, and Puerto Rican Americans may be better
able to keep the heritage cultures and languages alive.
However, might it be some basic differences in values that
promote these group differences?   For example, if we
examine the Kluckhohn value scores of the five ethnic
groups, we find sharp contrasts between the Arab American
parents and the Polish and Mexican Americans who are much
more alike on a series of dimensions.   Thus, the Arab
parents have a much stronger fatalistic outlook, an
extremely strong tendency to stay near one's parents, a
much stronger inclination to find work within an
organization, and, in comparison with the Mexican
Americans, a rejection of the idea of living for today
(item 7).   The unanswered question is whether these or
other value differences have a substantive effect on
heritage language and culture maintenance.   These
questions can only be addressed through further research
focused on various factors within and outside the family
that may or may not support the promotion of biculturality
and bilinguality through generations.
    Thus, it is one thing for parents to have hopes and
desires for heritage culture maintenance, but a different
and more demanding thing to make it work. What fascinates
us about the present study is that we have uncovered some
cases where it is working effectively and where it may
continue through generations, consequently satisfying
parental desires. At the same time, we have uncovered
other cases where it seems not to be working, consequently
leaving parental desires unsatisfied.

Introducing Heritage Languages into Public Schooling

    Events outside the family system sometimes transpire
that change   substantively the normal course of heritage
language usage. Sometimes outsiders can have a hand in
controlling such events.   In earlier chapters we have
shown that most ethnic groups in our study supported the

idea of introducing heritage languages on a part-time
basis in the public schools, although some suggested that
community or church-run classes could be equally good
alternatives. The underlying arguments for such public
school interventions are that use of the heritage language
in instruction can help language minority children grasp
new concepts through a familiar language, and thus
eliminate the typical falling behind in curriculum content.
In addition, using a heritage language in school even on a
part-time basis legitimizes the cultural background of the
children involved and thus enhances a sense of ethnic pride
and identity (see Lambert, 1981).   In this   study, we
learned that certain ethnic groups of parents would be
particularly pleased if such an intervention was possible.
The Puerto Rican American parents, for instance, give the
impression that Spanish should be offered as   a school
language for their children as a right of citizenship.
Arabic American parents give the impression that the
part-time use of Arabic in school would buttress their own
attempts to keep a precious heritage alive.
     What was critical for us in this endeavor was the
collaboration and encouragement we received from the
school superintendent and from the   directors of the
bilingual/bicultural educational program in the system.
With this support, an invitational letter was sent to
Arabic and Albanian parents and we were quickly assured
that sufficient numbers of grade 1 pupils would be
available for two pilot classes. Unfortunately, there was
no Albanian teacher available who had been educated in
that language and consequently the Albanian option was
delayed. There was, however, a teacher in the system who
was fluent in Arabic and who was delighted with the
opportunity to teach through his native language.   This
made the Arabic pilot project a reality.

An Arabic Partial Immersion Pilot Program

     The school principal supported the idea and permitted
a pilot "educational experiment" in Arabic partial
immersion to start for a small number of Grade 1 pupils.
The basic idea was that these pupils would be given an
opportunity to be educated through their home language for
half of each school day. The program was voluntary and
thus parents became involved from the start in planning
the curriculum. Here we report on the end-of-year

achievement outcomes for children who had such an educational experience.

We use the term "Arabic partial immersion" to indicate that Arabic is the major home language for the majority of pupils in the pilot group, although, interestingly enough, four fully Anglophone families registered their children for what they saw as an "enriching experience", and all but one have remained in the pilot class. Partial immersion refers to the fact that for each school day this subgroup of pupils moved to a separate room with a separate teacher for half the day, leaving the other half of the class in the homeroom with an English (only) speaking teacher who followed a conventional all English, standard curriculum for the full day. This group became our "comparison" or "control" group. Those who moved went to the Arabic immersion teacher and thus had half of their instruction presented exclusively through the Arabic language. This also meant that they had half as much time in an English language instructional atmosphere as did the pupils who stayed with the English speaking teacher, a point to remember in the evaluations to follow.

The Arabic speaking teacher using only the Arabic language concentrated on teaching all aspects of the content subjects required by the conventional curriculum. At the same time, the teacher reserved a restricted amount of instructional time for Arabic language arts. This was needed to maintain age-appropriate reading and writing skills in the language. In addition, since four pupils in the program did not have an Arabic language background, the language arts element in their case became crucial for the development of literacy skills in the language. Thus, the program was partially Arabic and partially English based, but there was no mixing of languages from either teacher; the instruction had a dual-language, two-teacher format.

Serious responsibilities fall to those who initiate or permit such a program to be implemented in a public school setting. Similar responsibilities fall to those who conduct evaluations of such programs. Our joint responsibility was to determine, as accurately as possible, whether minority language children (Arabic home language, in this case) are placed at a disadvantage in their schooling when attempts are made by school authorities to satisfy the wishes of parents to have their children cultivate a comfortable degree of bilingualism and biculturalism and to have the American public school system involved in the process. Thus, our major concern in the first-year pilot study was to determine as well as possible, with very small samples, if children from homes where Arabic is a major home language fall behind in their development of English language skills or in their mastery of curriculum content when half of their school day is spent in an Arabic language atmosphere. Our main point of comparison in this evaluation will be young children of the same age, same social class and same academic aptitude as those in the Arabic immersion program who have English as a home language and who follow an all-day English only curriculum. In this sense, the comparison was a demanding one since the comparison group had a conventional, full complement of English language instruction and had English as the only home language, placing them at an apparently very strong advantage. In time, other comparison groups will be brought into the design, especially other Arabic youngsters who do not have the opportunity to partake in such an Arabic immersion program.

Our reasoning in the present case was that minority language children may make great use of such an opportunity to develop bilingual/bicultural skills at the same time as their home language and culture are shown respect, since these were being introduced as part of their training in an American public school setting. On the basis of early research, we have argued that when such an opportunity is extended to minority language children, they and their families (1) have a sense of gratitude and appreciation to the host nation that provides the opportunity; (2) the children themselves are thereby motivated to become part of such a generous nation; (3) that their incipient bilingualism enhances their cognitive abilities; and (4) their likely prospects of losing the home language in competition with English (the "subtractive bilingualism" case) are ultimately transformed into prospects of becoming comfortably bilingual and bicultural (the "additive bilingualism" case) (see Lambert, 1984; Lambert & Taylor, 1983). Thus, it was not certain that the evaluation would show an ultimate advantage for the all-English comparison group.

Results as of the End of First Grade

The following tables present end-of-grade-one performance scores on English language tests for the two groups brought into comparison. There were eleven Arabic partial immersion and eleven English speaking comparison pupils.   First, we restricted our attention to the seven immersion pupils who had both parents with an Arabic language background.   Then, at the start of the school year, we tested the basic reasoning ability of each child by means of the Raven Progressive Matrices test, a procedure commonly used in cross-national research to predict children's readiness and likely capacity to deal with academic work.   An end-of-kindergarten form of the Metropolitan Achievement Test was also given at the start of the school year.

We were then in a position (1) to match the Arabic immersion pupils with seven comparison pupils in terms of initial Raven scores, and (2) to compare the two groups with a statistical correction (a covariance procedure) for initial differences in Raven scores.   The English language skills of prime interest were those measured by the Metropolitan Achievement Test (MAT).   Care was taken to use the appropriate age level of this test for pupils finishing grade one.

Table 7.3 presents the pretest and end-of-year test results without any matching or statistical corrections. It turned out that the Arabic immersion pupils scored below the English comparison pupils on the Raven test and the difference is statistically significant. This is difficult to explain.   It could mean that the Arab children were simply not accustomed to taking tests of this type or, since the Raven test has been found reliable in cross-national research, it could mean that the Arab children were less advanced cognitively than the comparison group controls. We favor the first alternative, but in any case it was clear that we had to equate the groups in terms of this important variable since the non-Arab pupils were significantly   stronger.   Nonetheless, without any statistical corrections, we found that the two groups were alike on pretest MAT scores; none of the differences was statistically significant.   Furthermore, even though at a disadvantage in terms of Raven scores, the Arab immersion pupils scored significantly higher than the comparison pupils on the end-of-year English reading subtest of the MAT and at the same level as the comparison pupils on all other subtests, namely, Mathematics, Language, Science, and Social Studies.

Tables 7. 4 and 7.5 show the performances of the two groups of pupils when the initial differences in Raven scores are eliminated through the statistical procedure of covariance. Again the same general outcomes were apparent: the Arab immersion pupils scored at the same level on all subtests of the MAT at the start of grade 1 and also at the end of grade 1, that is, after a full year of partial Arabic immersion that had taken them out of the English instruction atmosphere for half of each school day. At the end of the year, the immersion pupils score higher, by six score points, than the comparison pupils on the English reading subtest, although in this case the difference was not statistically significant. And again, the immerison pupils were at the same level as the comparison pupils on all other subtests given in English at the end of the year.

    In summary, the results of this pilot study permit us to conclude that the Arabic partial immersion experience has in no apparent way placed these minority language pupils in jeopardy in their development of English language skills nor in the other content matters included in the various end-of-year subtests of the MAT, all presented to the children in the form of English test questions. Thus, even though half of their instruction in Mathematics, Science, and Social Studies was given in Arabic, they perform as well on English tests of these matters as do the all-English, non-Arabic control children. Developing Arabic skills has, if anything, helped these pupils to and, in one instance, surpass English speaking pupils on end-of-year tests of achievement in grade one curriculum matters. This finding is consonant with our previous research on language minority students in other settings when they are given a chance to learn partly through their own language. The children in this case will be monitored as they proceed through grades, along with follow-up groups that will follow the same program one year behind them.

    No attempt was made in the first two years to explore how far these children have progressed in Arabic language skills. From observing them in class, however, there is no question that they process and use Arabic in a comfortable, natural way. The program, therefore, shows all the signs of fostering an effective form of bilingual and bicultural development for the children involved. What interests us in particular is that other neighboring districts in Michigan have begun to ask for similar programs in Arabic, Spanish, and Polish.

Arab Family Reactions to Arabic Partial Immersion

Our final research effort, also clearly exploratory in nature, was to investigate how the Arab American parents and their children in the immersion program feel about its effects, as of the end of the first grade. The seven families with children in the program were contacted, and one or both parents were more than willing to be interviewed. Interestingly, the male parents were by far the more prominent spokespersons for the family on this educational issue.

The questions asked each parent are presented in Table 7.6, along with the average parent responses. All of the parents indicated great satisfaction with the program; they expected much less from the program than actually transpired; they were very satisfied with their children's abilities to use both Arabic and English; they saw no problems in learning two languages, and instead, saw many advantages; they believed that their children enjoyed the program but no more the Arabic than the English half of it; they believed the Arabic schooling had helped in strengthening English language skills; they would very much like to see the program continued; and they would like all Arab children in the Detroit area to have the same opportunity. Clearly, the parents were very happy with the outcome of the experience and they view it as an educational adjunct that helps rather than competes with parallel English language development.

The pupils themselves were interviewed in a similar fashion; the questions asked them and the average responses are presented in Table 7.7. They definitely enjoyed having half-day schooling in Arabic, they also liked English classes very much; they would like to have even more time alloted to Arabic; they speak Arabic all or most of the time with family and sometimes with school friends outside class, and often in stores in town; when older, most would like to speak both English and Arabic; they see no ways in which learning Arabic hurts their progress in English, or vice versa; the majority never mix the two languages; and as a group they are very happy and proud to be Arabic, just as they are also very happy and proud to be "American". In sum, the children are very pleased with the program and, like their parents, see it as a separate, nonconflicting development in their lives. They also show signs of becoming comfortably Arabic as well as American, just what their parents had in mind for them from the start.

Table 7.1

Group Comparisons in Terms of Years Living in the United States

Ethnic Group	Years in Community	Years in America
Mexican American	21.73	39.13
Polish American	14.48	21.92
Arab American	9.15	10.31
Puerto Rican American	8.75	9.89
Albanian American	7.74	11.92
White Middle Class	19.72	37.92
White Working Class	19.33	42.72
Blacks - Pontiac	27.00	39.79
Blacks - Hamtramck	17.89	33.20

Table 7.2

Parents' Self-Ratings and Parents' Ratings of Children's Language
Fluency: Mean Scores

Parents' Self-Ratings	Fluency in Heritage Language	Fluency in English
Arab American	6.86	5.07
Puerto Rican American	6.83	3.98
Mexican American	5.78	5.95
Albanian American	5.78	3.48
Polish American	3.84	5.19

Parents' Ratings of Children	Fluency in Heritage Language	Fluency in English
Arab American	6.87	6.49
Puerto Rican American	6.71	5.93
Albanian American	5.69	5.87
Mexican American	3.08	6.28
Polish American	2.38	5.82

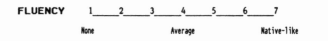

FLUENCY   1____2____3____4____5____6____7
           None   Average   Native-like

Table 7.3

Mean Scores on MAT Tests at Start and End of Grade 1

Arabic Partial Immersion Versus All English Control Pupils:
Unmatched on Raven Test

	Arabic Partial Immersion Pupils (n = 7)	English Speaking Control Pupils (n = 11)	F-Ratio	df
Raven (36)*	12.57	16.18	6.47*	1,16
Fall Testing of MAT				
Reading (55)	7.57	10.45	0.64	1,16
Mathematics (40)	11.43	10.73	0.13	1,16
Language (40)	10.14	11.00	0.12	1,16
End of Year Testing of MAT				
Reading	26.29	18.78 (n=9)	4.59*	1,14
Mathematics	23.86	21.45	2.06	1,16
Language	25.43	24.36	0.18	1,16
Science	29.86	31.18	1.57	1,16
Social Studies	25.71	26.09	0.04	1,16

* The total possible scores are given in parentheses.
* Indicates a non-chance, statistically reliable difference in group mean scores.

181

Table 7.4

Adjusted Mean Scores

Group Comparisons with Pupils Matched on Raven Scores

	Arabic Partial Immersion Pupils (n = 6)	English Speaking Control Pupils (n = 6)	F-Ratio	d-f
Raven (36)	12.83	13.67	0.47	1,10
Fall Testing of MAT				
Reading (55)	7.67	7.50	0.00	1,10
Mathematics (40)	10.67	10.33	0.03	1,16
Language (40)	8.83	9.67	0.08	1,10
End of Year Testing of MAT				
Reading	23.50	19.60 (n=5)	1.31	1,09
Mathematics	23.00	20.67	2.29	1,10
Language	24.50	25.83	0.24	1,10
Science	29.50	31.00	1.06	1,10
Social Studies	25.33	26.00	0.07	1,10

Table 7.5

Adjusted Mean Scores

Group Comparisons with Raven Scores Controlled by Covariance

	Arabic Partial Immersion Pupils (n = 7)	English Speaking Control Pupils (n = 11)	F-Ratio	d-f
Fall Testing of MAT				
Reading	9.01	9.54	0.09	1,15
Mathematics	11.59	10.62	0.17	1,15
Language	10.47	10.80	0.01	1,15
End of Year Testing of MAT				
Reading	25.89	19.08 (n=9)	2.68	1,13
Mathematics	24.22	21.23	2.21	1,15
Language	23.60	25.53	0.53	1,15
Science	29.61	31.35	1.89	1,15
Social Studies	25.82	26.02	0.01	1,15

Table 7.6

Responses of Arab American Parents About the
Arabic Immersion Program

1. In general, are you satisfied or dissatisfied
    with the program of Arabic instruction your
    child is now receiving?   Mean Score = 7.00

         Dissatisfied 1___2___3___4___5___6___7 Satisfied
                       Very   Neutral   Very

---

2. Did you expect more or less from the Arab
    program for your child?   Mean Score = 5.85

         Expected 1___2___3___4___5___6___7 Expected
           More   Less
               A lot more   Neutral   A lot less

---

3. Are you satisfied or dissatisfied with your
    child's ability to use Arabic?   Mean Score = 6.85

         Dissatisfied 1___2___3___4___5___6___7 Satisfied
                       Very   Neutral   Very

---

4. Are you satisfied or dissatisfied with your
    child's ability to use English?   Mean Score = 6.71

         Dissatisfied 1___2___3___4___5___6___7 Satisfied
                       Very   Neutral   Very

---

5. Does your child enjoy learning through Arabic
    or does he/she dislike it?   Mean Score = 6.85

         Dislikes 1___2___3___4___5___6___7 Likes
                               Neutral

184

6. Does your child prefer Arabic or English
classes?   Mean Score = 3.28

Likes   1____ 2____ 3____ 4____ 5____ 6____ 7   Likes
         ↑   ↑   ↑
    English much   Neutral   Arabic much
    more than Arabic   more than English

---

7. Has learning through Arabic half day
hindered your child's progress in
English or not?   Mean Score = 5.71

Hindered
His/Her   1____ 2____ 3____ 4____ 5____ 6____ 7   Helped
English   ↑   ↑   ↑   His/Her
        Very much   Neutral   Very much   English

---

8. Would you be happy or disappointed if
your child had a similar half day Arab
program next year for grade 2?   Mean Score = 7.00

Disappointed 1____ 2____ 3____ 4____ 5____ 6____ 7 Happy
               ↑   ↑   ↑
              Very   Neutral   Very

Table 7.7

Response of Pupils About Arabic Immersion Program

1.   Do you like having half day school in Arabic?

Mean Score = 1.15

Like 1___2___3___4___5 Dislike
      A lot   Not Sure   A lot

---

2.   Do you like having English classes?   Mean Score = 1.43

Like 1___2___3___4___5 Dislike
      A lot   Not Sure   A Lot

---

3.   Would you like your school to spend more
      time or less on Arabic?   Mean Score = 1.85

Time on   Time on
Arabic 1___2___3___4___5 Arabic
      Much more   Equal Amount   Much Less

---

4.   Do you speak Arabic with your family?   Mean Score = 1.15

Yes 1___2___3___4___5 No
              Occasionally

---

5.   Do you speak Arabic with your school friends
      outside of class?   Mean Score = 1.71

Yes 1___2___3___4___5 No
              Occasionally

---

6.   Do you speak Arabic in stores in town?   Mean Scores = 1.43

Yes 1___2___3___4___5 No
              Occasionally

186

7. When you are older, which would you
    like most?   <u>Mean Score</u> = 5c's; 1a's; 1b

    a) to speak mostly   b) to speak mostly   c) to speak
        English; just a   Arabic; just a   <u>both</u> English
        little Arabic   little English   and Arabic

---

8. If you learn Arabic, does it bother/hurt
    your English?   <u>Mean Score</u> = 5.00

            Yes ¹___²___³___⁴___⁵ No
                         ↑
                     Not Sure

---

9. If you learn English, does it bother/hurt
    your Arabic?   <u>Mean Score</u> = 5.00

            Yes ¹___²___³___⁴___⁵ No
                         ↑
                    Occasionally

---

10. Are you happy, proud, to be Arab?   <u>Mean Score</u> = 1.15

            Yes ¹___²___³___⁴___⁵ No
                      ↑
                    So-So

---

11. Are you happy, proud, to be American?   <u>Mean Score</u> = 1.43

            Yes ¹___²___³___⁴___⁵ No
                      ↑
                    So-So

187

Bibliography

Abramson, H.J. 1973. Ethnic diversity in Catholic America. NY: Wiley.

Adorno, T.W., Frenkel-Brunswick, E., Levinson, D.J., and Sanford, R.N. 1950. The authoritarian personality. New York, NY: Harper and Row.

Aellen, C. and Lambert, W.E. 1969. Ethnic identification and personality adjustments of Canadian adolescents of mixed English-French parentage. Canadian Journal of Behavioural Science, 1, 69-86.

Alba, R. 1981. The twilight of ethnicity among American Catholics of European ancestry. The Annals, American Academy of Political and Social Science, 454, 86-97.

Allport, G.W. 1954. The nature of prejudice. Boston, MA: Beacon Press.

Amiel, B. 1984. The blooming of hypocrisy. Maclean's, December 24, p. 7.

Anderson, E.L. 1938. We Americans. Cambridge, MA: Harvard University Press.

Angle, J.   1976.   Mainland control of manufacturing and reward for bilingualism in Puerto Rico.   American Sociological Review, 41, 289-307.

Berry, J.W., Kalin, R., and Taylor, D.M.   1977. Multiculturalism and ethnic attitudes in Canada. Ottawa, Minister of Supply and Services.

Breton, R.   1978.   Stratification and conflict between ethnolinguistic communities with different social structures.   Canadian Review of Sociology and Anthropology, 15, 148-157.

Byrne, D.   1971.   The attraction paradigm.   New York: Academic Press.

Cohen, A.   1969.   Custom and politics in urban Africa. Berkeley, CA: University of California Press.

Collins, G.   1985.   A new look at intermarriage in the U.S. The New York Times,   February 11.

Coser, L.A., Nock, S.L., Steffan, P.A., and Rhea, B.   1987. Introduction to Sociology.   New York, NY: Harcourt, Brace, Jovanovich.

Cunningham, S.   1984.   Culture plays important role in our beliefs.   American Psychological Association Monitor, 15 (9), 8-9.

Danzig, D.   1964.   The meaning of Negro strategy. Commentary, 37, 36-44.

Durkheim, E.   [1893] 1949.   Division of labour in society. Glencoe, IL: Free Press.

Enloe, C.   1980.   Ethnic soldiers.   Athens, GA: University of Georgia Press.

Esman, M.J.   1987.   Politics and economic power. Comparative Politics, 19, 395-417.

Ferguson, G.A.   1981.   Statistical analysis in psychology and education.   New York, NY: McGraw Hill.

Gans, H.J. 1962. The urban villagers. New York, NY: The
    Free Press.

Gans, H.J. 1979. Symbolic ethnicity: The future of
    ethnic groups and cultures in America. Ethnic and
    Racial Studies, 2, 1-20.

Genesee, F. 1984. Historical and theoretical foundations
    of immersion education. In Studies on immersion
    education: A collection for United States educators.
    Sacramento: California State Department of Education.

Giles, H., Taylor, D.M., and Bourhis, R.Y. 1972.
    Dimensions of Welsh identity. European Journal of
    Social Psychology, 7, 165-174.

Glazer, N. and Moynihan, D.P. 1970. Beyond the melting
    pot. Cambridge, MA: M.I.T. Press.

Gordon, M.M. 1961. Assimilation in America: Theory and
    reality. Daedalus, Spring, 263-285.

Gordon, M.M. 1964. Assimilation in American life: The
    role of race, religion and national origins. New York:
    NY: Oxford University Press.

Gordon, M.M. 1981. Models of pluralism: The new American
    dilemma. The Annals, American Academy of Political and
    Social Science, 454, 178-188.

Greeley, A. 1974. Ethnicity in the United States. New
    York, NY: Wiley.

Grittner, F.M. 1987. Public policies and ethnic
    influences upon foreign language study in the public
    schools. In Van Horne, W.A. and Tonnesen, T.V. Eds.,
    Ethnicity and language. Wisconsin: The University of
    Wisconsin System Institute on Race and Ethnicity, 189-
    211.

Hamburg, D.A. 1984. Prejudice, ethnocentrism, and
    violence in an age of high technology. Annual Report
    1984. New York: NY: Carnegie Corporation of New York.

Hechter, M.   1974.   The political economy of ethnic change. American Journal of Sociology, 79, 1151-1178.

Hechter, M.   1977.   International colonialism: The Celtic fringe in British national development, 1536-1966. Berkeley: University of California Press.

Isajiw, W.W.   1983.   Multiculturalism and the integration of the Canadian community.   Canadian Ethnic Studies, 83, 107-117.

Jones, H.M.   1944.   Ideas in America.   Cambridge, MA: Harvard University Press.

Jones, F. and Lambert, W.E.   1959.   Attitudes toward immigrants in a Canadian community.   Public Opinion Quarterly, 23, 537-546.

Jones, F. and Lambert, W.E.   1965.   Occupational rank and attitudes toward immigrants. Public Opinion Quarterly, 29, 137-144.

Jones, F. and Lambert, W.E.   1967.   Some situational influences on attitudes toward immigrants.   British Journal of Sociology, 18, 408-424.

Kandel, D.B.   1978.   Similarity in real-life adolescent friendship pairs.   Journal of Personality and Social Psychology, 36, 306-312.

Kasfir, N.   1979.   Explaining ethnic political participation. World Politics, 31, 365-388.

Kluckhohn, F.   1950.   Dominant and substitute profiles of cultural orientations. Social Forces, 28, 376-393.

Kolodny, R.   1969.   Ethnic cleavages in the United States: An historical reminder to social workers.   Social Work, 14, 13-23.

Lahne, H.   1944.   The cotton mill worker.   New York: NY: Farrar and Rinehart.

Lambert, R.D. 1981. Ethnic/racial relations in the United States in comparative perspective. The Annals, American Academy of Political and Social Science, 454, 189-206.

Lambert, W.E. 1952. Comparison of French and American modes of response to the Bogardus Social Distance Scale. Social Forces, 31, 155-160.

Lambert, W.E. 1967. A social psychology of bilingualism. Social Issues, 23, 91-109.

Lambert, W.E. 1981. Bilingualism and language acquisition. In Winitz, H. Ed., Native language and foreign language acquisition, New York, NY: The New York Academy of Sciences.

Lambert, W.E. 1984. An overview of issues in immersion education. In Studies on immersion education: A collection for United States educators. Sacramento: California State Department of Education.

Lambert, W.E. 1987. The effects of bilingual and bicultural experiences on children's attitudes and social perspectives. In Hamel, P., Palij, M., and Aaronson, D. Eds., Childhood bilingualism. Hillsdale, NJ: Lawrence Erlbaum, 197-222.

Lambert, W.E. 1988. "Minority" Language Rights and Education in Quebec. Paper for conference on Minority Language Rights and Education, Cornell University, May, 1988.

Lambert, W.E. and Klineberg, O. 1967. Children's views of foreign peoples: A cross-national study. NY: Appleton-Century-Crofts.

Lambert, W.E., Mermigis, L., and Taylor, D.M.. 1986. Greek Canadians' attitudes toward own group and other Canadian ethnic groups: A test of the multiculturalism hypothesis. The Canadian Journal of Behavioral Sciences, 18, 35-51.

Lambert, W.E. and Taylor, D.M. 1983. Language in the education of ethnic minority immigrants. In Samuda, R.J. and Woods, S.L. Eds., Perspectives in immigrant and minority education. Washington, DC: University Press of America.

Lambert, W.E. and Taylor, D.M. 1987. Language minorities in the United States: Conflicts around assimilation and proposed modes of accomodation. In Van Horne, W.A. and Tonnesen, T.V. Eds., Ethnicity and language. Madison, WI: The University of Wisconsin System.

Lambert, W.E. and Tucker, G.R. 1972. Bilingual education of children. Rowley, MA: Newbury House.

Levine, R.A. and Campbell, D.T. 1972. Ethnocentrism. New York, NY: Wiley & Sons.

Marx, K. [1867] 1967. Capital. 3 vols. New York: NY: International Publishers.

McClelland, D.C. 1961. The achieving society. New York, NY: Van Nostrand.

Moe, J.L., Nacoste, R.W., and Insko, C.A. 1981. Belief versus race as determinants of discrimination: A study of southern adolescents in 1966 and 1979. Journal of Personality and Social Psychology, 41, 1031-1050.

Morse, N. and Allport, F.H. 1952. The causation of anti-Semitism. Journal of Psychology, 34, 225-236.

Myrdal, G. 1944. An American dilemma. New York, NY: Harper & Bros.

Nagel, J. 1982. The political mobilization of native Americans. Social Science Journal, 19, 37-46.

Nagel, J. and Olzak, S. 1982. Ethnic mobilization in new and old states: An extension of the competition model. Social Problems, 30, 127-143.

Newcomb, T.M. 1961. The acquaintance process. New York, NY: Holt, Rinehart and Winston.

Nielsen, F.   1986.   The Flemish movement in Belgium after World War II. American Sociological Review, 45, 76-94.

Olzak, S.   1982.   Ethnic mobilization in Quebec. Ethnic and Racial Studies, 5, 253-275.

Pachon, H.P. and Moore, J.W.   1981.   Mexican Americans.   In Gordon, M.M. Ed., America as a multicultural society. Philadephia: The Annals (American Academy of Political and Social Science), 454, 111-124.

Park, R.E.   1928.   Human migration and the marginal man. American Journal of Sociology, May, 881-893.

Park, R.E. and Burgess, E.W.   1921.   Introduction to the science of society.   Chicago: University of Chicago Press.

Perlez, J.   1983.   Moynihan and Glazer feel vindicated. New York Times, December 3.

Portes, A.   1984.   The rise of ethnicity: Determinants of ethnic perceptions among Cuban exiles in Miami. American Sociological Review, 49, 383-397.

Rosen, B.C.   1959.   Race, ethnicity, and the achievement syndrome. American Sociological Review, 24, 47-60.

Rosen, B.C. and D'Andrade, R.   1959.   The psychosocial origins of achievement motive.   Sociometry, 22, 185-218.

Siegel, S.   1956.   Nonparametric statistics. New York, NY: McGraw Hill.

Silverman, B.I., and Cochrane, R.   1972.   Effects of social context on the principles of belief congruence. Journal of Personality and Social Psychology, 22, 259-268.

Sowell, T.   1983.   The economics and politics of race. New York, NY: W. Morrow and Co.

Taylor, D.M.   1987.   Social psychological barriers to
    effective childhood bilingualism.   In Hamel, P., Palij,
    F.M., and Aaronson, D. Eds.,   Childhood bilingualism:
    Aspects of cognitive, social and emotional development.
    New Jersey: Erlbaum Associates, 183-195.

Taylor, D.M., Bassili, J., and Aboud, F.E.   1973.
    Dimensions of ethnic identity: An example from Quebec.
    Journal of Social Psychology, 89, 185-192.

Taylor, D.M., and Simard, L.   1975.   Social interaction in
    a bilingual setting.   Canadian Psychological Review,
    16, 230-254.

Taylor, D.M., Meynard, R., and Rheault, E.   1977.   Threat
    to ethnic identity and second-language learning.   In
    Giles, H. Ed., Language, ethnicity, and intergroup
    relations. London: Academic Press.

Taylor, D.M., and McKirnan, D.J.   1984.   A five-stage model
    of intergroup relations.   British Journal of Social
    Psychology, 23, 291-300.

Trudeau, P.E.   1971.   Statement by the Prime Minister
    (Response to the Report of the Royal Commission on
    Bilingualism and Biculturalism, Book 4, House of
    Commons).   Government of Canada.   Ottawa: Press
    Release, October 8, 1971.

Tucker, G.R.   1980.   Comments on proposed rules for non
    discrimination under programs receiving federal
    financial assistance through the Education Department.
    Washington, DC: Center for Applied Linguistics.

Warne, F.J.   1913.   The immigrant invasion.   New York, NY:
    Dodd, Meade & Co.

Warner, W.L. and Srole, L.   1945.   The social systems of
    American ethnic groups.   New Haven: Yale University
    Press.

Wolfe, L.   1985.   Moynihan, as a Fellow at Columbia, revels
    in a return to campus life.   The New York Times,
    February 26, 1985, p. 31.

Wolfe, T.   1987.   The bonfire of the vanities.   New York,
    NY: Farrar, Straus and Giroux.

Yancey, W., Ericksen, E., and Juliani, R.   1976.   Emergent
    ethnicity: A review and reformulation.   American
    Sociological Review, 41, 391-403.

Young, D.R. 1932.   American minority peoples.   New York,
    NY: Harper.

Zangwill, I.   1914.   The melting pot: Drama in four acts.
    New York, NY: Macmillan.

Index

ABOUT THE AUTHORS

Wallace E. Lambert is a professor of psychology at McGill University with research interests in social and experimental psychology, cross-national studies, and psycho- and socio-linguistics. These are reflected in numerous publications, including Social Psychology, a textbook written in collaboration with his brother, William W. Lambert; Children's Views of Foreign Peoples: A Cross National Study, with Otto Klineberg; Bilingual Education of Children: The St. Lambert Experiment; Tu, Vous, Usted: A Social Psychology of Forms of Address; French Speakers' Skill with Grammatical Gender: An Example of Rule-Governed Behavior, all three in collaboration with Richard G. Tucker; Attitudes and Motivation in Second Language Learning in collaboration with Robert C. Gardner; Language, Psychology and Culture: Essays by W.E. Lambert, edited by A.S. Dil; and Child Rearing Values: A Cross-National Study, with Josiane Hamers and Nancy Frasure Smith.

Donald M. Taylor is a professor of psychology at McGill University. Professor Taylor's research interest is in intergroup relations, including such topics as ethnic stereotypes, intergroup communication, ethnic identity, and multicultural societies. His research has been conducted in diverse regions of the world, including the United States, Canada, Britain, South and South-East Asia. Professor Taylor has contributed numerous articles in Canadian, American, European, and Asian journals, co-authored a major work on multiculturalism titled Multiculturalism and Ethnic Attitudes in Canada with J.W. Berry and R. Kalin, and more recently, a book in collaboration with F.M. Moghaddam titled Theories of Intergroup Relations. He also serves on the editorial board of a number of scientific journals.